The Spice Collector's Cookbook

The Spice Collector's Cookbook

Easy family recipes
inspired by spices from
across the globe

Vina Thakkar Patel

Recipe photography by Jonathan Lovekin

NOURISH

EAT WELL, LIVE WELL

To Haresh, Elissa, Aamir and Ravina, My Mom, and Sir Richard Parker (Pappu, our Golden Retriever)

✤ ✤ ✤ ✤ ✤ ✤ ✤ ✤ ✤ ✤ ✤ ✤ ✤ ✤ ✤ ✤

THE SPICE COLLECTOR'S COOKBOOK
Vina Thakkar Patel

First published in the UK and USA in 2024 by
Nourish, an imprint of Watkins Media Limited
Unit 11, Shepperton House, 83–93 Shepperton Road,
London N1 3DF

enquiries@nourishbooks.com

Agent: Monica Meehan at the Monica Meehan Agency
Publisher: Fiona Robertson
Commissioning Editor: Ella Chappell
Copyeditor: Rebecca Woods
Head of Design: Karen Smith
Production: Uzma Taj
Commissioned photography: Jonathan Lovekin
Food & Prop Stylist: Elissa Patel

A CIP record for this book is available from the
British Library

ISBN: 978–1–84899–429–4 (Hardback)
ISBN:978–1–84899–430–0 (eBook)

10 9 8 7 6 5 4 3 2 1

Typeset in Madela, Adobe Caslon Pro and Cera
Printed in China

Publisher's note
While every care has been taken in compiling the
recipes for this book, Watkins Media Limited, or any
other persons who have been involved in working on
this publication, cannot accept responsibility for any
errors or omissions, inadvertent or not, that may be
found in the recipes or text, nor for any problems that
may arise as a result of preparing one of these recipes.
If you are pregnant or breastfeeding or have any
special dietary requirements or medical conditions, it
is advisable to consult a medical professional before
following any of the recipes contained in this book.

Notes on the recipes
Unless otherwise stated:
Use vegetable or corn oil
Use medium fruit and vegetables
Use fresh herbs, spices and chilies
Do not mix metric, imperial and US cup
measurements:
1 tsp = 5ml 1 tbsp = 15ml 1 cup = 240ml

nourishbooks.com

Contents

Introduction

About me

My family's culinary and spice collecting journey began generations ago in the spice trade in Gujarat, India, long before my birth. My grandparents owned a spice shop that sold spices and grains to all the residents and neighboring towns. My grandmother was a progressive and aggressive woman in the early 1900s, which is probably where I got my spunk from. Women in those days did not work in the business, but my grandmother wanted to help my grandfather's spice shop thrive, so she made an elaborate recipe called Handvo (which is included in my first cookbook *From Gujarat with Love*). All the customers loved the Handvo and asked for the recipe. With the recipe in hand, customers bought a lot of the spices from the shop. My grandmother made their business thrive. She was way ahead of her time, as she figured out that by giving away samples, you can sell more groceries. A lot of big grocery stores use that technique today!

Spices are in my DNA. My town is all about spice shops, since it is a small trading hub for spices and grains. My father opened up and ran a successful business in trading grain and rice and eventually opened up a food-processing mill. As a young girl, I would play with all the grain and spices there and make a huge mess. He never got angry with me. My older brother was much older than me, so I pretty much grew up with my nieces and nephews. I had a grandmother, a mother, two older sisters, and two sisters-in-law who did all the cooking so I never had to learn how to cook. Everything was served to me on a silver platter, but I kept a watchful eye on what they were doing in the kitchen.

It wasn't until I got married at the age of 22 and moved to the US over 30 years ago that I had to learn everything from scratch for my super-foodie husband. I was horrified to see cans and jars of pre-made food on the grocery store shelves. When my children came along, I promised myself that I would not feed them any processed food. I was tasked with cooking healthy and delicious meals for my family in my Californian kitchen.

I wanted my children exposed to authentic Gujarati food and insisted on bringing the taste of home-cooked Gujarati food to my kitchen so they could experience it. But raising my kids in the US meant they developed a taste for different food that wasn't Indian and thus I was forced to get out of my comfort zone. I worked hard to discourage them from eating junk food, which is why I often tell them that a healthy, home-cooked meal can often take the same amount of time as going to collect a takeaway. More so, as a mother (and a wife), I care deeply about the emotional and physical benefits of gathering as a family at mealtimes. If we can put those delivery apps away, and instead connect while enjoying a home-cooked meal that boasts fresh ingredients (and that's

made with love – the most important ingredient),
I know my job is done. This was my main inspiration
for this book.

These recipes will take you on a journey across the
world. Many amazing people carried me on this
journey and taught me so much more than I ever
thought possible. My toughest critics are still my kids,
and they warm my heart when they tell me my food is
better than a restaurant! These compliments never grow
old; instead, they continue to encourage me to learn
more and get better.

> "Once you have
> found a recipe
> you love and
> have perfected
> it over time, try
> switching things
> up a bit and play
> around with
> ingredients."

My cooking philosophy

I believe we should all approach cooking in the same manner. Once you have found
a recipe you love and have perfected it over time, try switching things up a bit and
play around with ingredients. Cooking shouldn't be seen as something ritualistic or
overwhelming; it can be a wonderful, creative way to decompress after a stressful day.

I have gained my strength through food. You will see how each one of my recipes has
created many amazing dinners for my family and friends. The recipes in this book are
fast and easy to follow. Most can be made in less than 10–15 minutes. They are healthy
and packed with nutrients, because it's important to care about what we are putting into
our bodies.

Cooking with different ingredients and flavors is – in my opinion – a fabulous way to
develop taste buds while learning something new. So, I have sourced and perfected the
most popular family favorites here – and I am confident that even the fussiest of eaters
will enjoy the exotic flavors on every page.

I want to now encourage you to allow your creations on your dinner table to be varied.
As we are all aware, keeping meals exciting and interesting adds to the "spice" of life,
and this is best done by enjoying a wide variety of food and cuisines.

My passion for no-rules "fusion" cooking

I grew up eating mostly Indian food – with the occasional pizza with tomato ketchup, Asian soup, noodles, and egg rolls. After relocating to the US, my husband introduced me to many different cuisines, but I was a very picky eater and simply not interested in anything that smelled or tasted remotely "unfamiliar" to me. I even recall wanting only rice with chili sauce on many occasions in those early days: nothing else enticed me! To remedy this bizarre situation we found ourselves in, we chose to only visit restaurants when I was very hungry: this forced me to slowly start picking at food that was unfamiliar to my palate!

Soon enough, however, our family grew – and making home-cooked meals became my priority. Our children's palate was different to my own, so I strongly invested my time and energy in finding ways to present them with non-Indian food that was still healthy and satisfying. Enjoying long lunches with other American mothers and plenty of dinner parties with friends helped me: I learned about ingredients I was not familiar with, and then found exciting ways to replicate these dishes (with my own Vina-modifications, of course!).

While this change was happening at home, we also began to travel regularly around the world. I have now visited 36 countries and counting! When traveling, I always make it a priority to discover the finer details of what went into a meal I enjoyed. Some cooks and chefs from the establishments were generous in sharing their tips, while others left me to my own devices to go back into my kitchen and recreate it from memory alone.

But fusion cooking is not just about replicating recipes from other places. When traveling as a family, we find ourselves craving Indian food after a few days in Italy, or an Italian meal after a few days in India! This is not surprising since one needs a little variety in life, and even at home after a few days of my homemade Gujarati meals, there will be requests for something Mexican or Thai. In our globalized world, Gujarati families can cook their local dishes in Venice, while an Italian family may try aubergine chaat in Milan, each tweaking the recipes to suit their available ingredients and personal tastes.

I've found authentic Italian recipes not just on my many trips to Italy but all over the world and in the oddest locations, such as Rio, Brazil, Napa Valley and Silicon Valley, California, Santa Teresa, Costa Rica, and Vadodara, Mumbai, Delhi, Rajasthan and Goa, India. This is because everyone loves Italian food, and a lot of Italian immigrants open restaurants. The same goes for Chinese, Thai, Mexican and hundreds of other cultures and peoples.

On my second trip to the Amalfi coast in 2016, I met a lovely person sitting next to me at the airport who overheard our conversations about the food we'd eaten. She told me about her cooking class in Priano and finding the best pizza recipe. She shared it with me. I have been using that recipe for over nine years – an authentic pizza recipe, communicated at an airport in Italy and transported back to Silicon Valley. There really are no rules when it comes to food!

At an Italian restaurant in Costa Rica, I asked for ravioli with marinara sauce instead of butter sage sauce, which was the "special of the day". The co-owner, who was also the chef's wife, offered to bring out the marinara sauce separately so we could mix it ourselves because her stubborn Sicilian husband refused to modify the special on the menu. The marinara sauce was so good that we had to compliment the chef. We made peace at the end of the evening and the couple invited us round the next day, to teach me how to make the world's best marinara sauce. You'll find a picture of the three of us in the book.

There are so many recipes I could share in this book, but I have settled on Indian, Thai, Mexican and Italian food as the four main cuisines I focus on, along with some of the world's best salads. I have selected these because they are the ones my family enjoys most. Each recipe has its own story which you'll find interesting and humorous.

I hope you enjoy them all as much as my family and friends do!

"Allow your creations on your dinner table to be varied, because keeping meal times diverse is very important ... keeping meals exciting and interesting adds to the 'spice' of life."

Storecupboard Essentials

❧ ❧ ❧ ❧ ❧ ❧ ❧ ❧ ❧ ❧ ❧ ❧ ❧ ❧ ❧

HEALTHY INGREDIENTS ARE KEY

I respect the ingredients I use, not just because they are delicious but because they are healthy and nutritious in many ways. Here are some ingredients you will find throughout this book and some of their incredible health benefits:

❧ Amla *(Indian gooseberry)*
Amla, also known as Indian gooseberry, is rich in vitamin C and promotes digestion and stabilizes blood sugar levels. It also improves your skin and hair health. Adding it to your diet can naturally boost your overall health. You can use amla for various purposes such as making pickles or a healthy drink (see page 177). Adding amla powder to your diet can be an easy way to enjoy its benefits. Amla can also be bought frozen.

❧ Basil *(Thai, sweet and normal)*
Thai basil has a stronger aroma and flavor than sweet basil. It is native to Southeast Asia, and is used in curries, soups and rice dishes in Thailand and Vietnam. As a leafy green, it has medicinal properties. If you cook without basil, you'll certainly notice the difference in taste. Thai cuisine loses its essence without the addition of these bright green leaves.

Here is one of my culinary secrets, though: if I can't find Thai basil, I use normal basil – in fact, I use both interchangeably! So don't worry if you can't find one or the other – the flavor notes are similar enough to use whichever type of basil you can get your hands on.

❧ Besan *(gram/chickpea flour)*
Besan, also known as chickpea flour or gram flour, is a special ingredient close to my heart. It is a staple ingredient in every Indian kitchen, and most Gujarati snacks are made with besan. I have fond memories of playing with besan at my dad's processing mill as a child.

❧ Black-eyed peas
With their buttery taste and creamy texture, black-eyes peas can be a delicious addition to any vegan or vegetarian diet. Their versatility makes them a kitchen staple. In addition to being nutritious and satisfying, I adore their appearance too, with the contrast of cream color and the distinctive black spot.

❧ Cardamom
Cardamom is a versatile spice used in cooking. It has a sweet aroma and is used in garam masala, tea masala, and sweet dishes. It has anti-inflammatory properties that help reduce inflammation and pain in the body. In India, cardamom seeds are used as a mouth freshener. Indian sweet dishes are incomplete without cardamom.

❧ Cayenne pepper

Cayenne pepper is a variety of spicy chili powder renowned for its vibrant color and strong flavor. It contains capsaicin, which can help boost the metabolism and reduce appetite, among other benefits. It is mainly used to enhance the flavor and appearance of dal curry soup. Cayenne peppers grow best in hot and sunny climates.

❧ Coarse semolina *(sooji or suji)*

This coarse flour made from durum wheat can vary in color from yellow to white depending on the quality of the grain. The fibre content in semolina means it is digested slowly, keeping your stomach full and preventing overeating. It also improves kidney function because of its potassium content.

❧ Coconut

The white flesh of this popular tropical fruit can be eaten raw; it has a natural sweetness and a chewy, firm texture. It is often used in many forms in both baking and cooking. Coconut is packed with important nutrients such as vitamins, minerals and healthy fats. Coconut milk and oil are commonly used in culinary cultures across the world, especially in Thailand and southern India.

❧ Coriander seeds and powder

Coriander seeds are often used in spice blends. They are easy to grind and add to your cooking. These seeds are also known for their digestive properties and are a good source of dietary fiber, vitamin C, and minerals.

❧ Cumin *(jeera)*

I grew up in Gujarat, and as a child I had the opportunity to visit Unjha, a district in North Gujarat famous for growing tons of cumin seeds that are supplied all over India and abroad. The seeds are harvested around the festival of Holi in March. Cumin seeds have a warm, sharp and earthy flavor and are an integral part of Indian cooking. The whole seeds are used for tempering or seasoning. To make this seasoning, known as tadka, the seeds are cooked in hot oil or ghee to infuse the oil with their flavor before pouring over the dish. Roasted cumin seed powder is commonly sprinkled over raita before serving. It has a very sharp and strong aroma that wafts through your house. The seeds are rich in iron and incorporating them into your diet helps support your immune system.

❧ Curry leaves

Curry leaves offer many health benefits and flavors. If you have some outdoor space, they are ideal for growing at home. I have a small plant, and it is much more fun to pick the leaves in my backyard than buy them from the store. However, they are also readily available at most supermarkets or at Indian supermarkets.

❧ Fenugreek *(methi)* seeds

These seeds are excellent for treating health issues like diabetes and digestive ailments. Soaked fenugreek seeds can be consumed on an empty stomach to relieve acidity and keep gastritis at bay. Methi dana, or fenugreek water, is terrific for regulating blood sugar, so it's very beneficial for people with diabetes. Sprouted fenugreek is even better, as it has 30-40% more nutritional properties than soaked fenugreek seeds and is more tolerable to the palate. Soaked or sprouted fenugreek seeds can help lower high cholesterol levels.

❧ Ginger

This spice is excellent for building immunity since it is enriched with antioxidants and anti-inflammatory properties. In addition, it is a traditional remedy for digestion.

❧ Ground coriander-cumin powder

This is a generic powder used mainly in Gujarati dishes. It is often called the "Magic Potion of Gujarati Cooking." Coriander seeds, also known as *dhania* in Hindi and *dhana* in Gujarati, are among the most popular spices used in almost all cuisines across India for their pleasant flavor. In Ayurveda, they are highly recommended for their various health benefits, such as controlling blood sugar levels in diabetes and aiding digestion. Coriander seeds have antioxidant properties and contain dietary fiber which promote healthy liver function and bowel movements. You can buy this pre-made mixture at Indian supermarkets, or you can make your own at home very easily with this simple recipe:

Coriander-cumin powder is also known as *dhana jeeru*. To make this spice mix, all you need is two ingredients: coriander seeds and cumin seeds.

Ingredients:
75g/2¾oz/1 cup coriander seeds
2 tbsp cumin seeds

Method:
Heat a frying pan or skillet over a low heat. Add the cumin seeds and dry roast for 3–5 minutes, stirring constantly. Take off the heat and set aside to cool completely.

Combine both seeds in a blender and blitz to a smooth powder. It can be stored in an airtight container for up to one year.

❧ Jaggery *(Gur)*

Jaggery is a sweetener made from boiled sugarcane juice. It has an earthy taste and is commonly used in Gujarati cuisine. For Gujaratis, jaggery is an essential ingredient, as our cuisine has a balance of sweet and sour flavors. Without jaggery, our food would lose its essence.

❧ Kashmiri chili powder

This chili powder adds flavor to curry and dal. It is less spicy than other chili powders, but one of the most remarkable aspects about Kashmiri chili powder is its vibrant color. It is known for its ability to visually enhance dishes; when added to a hot oil, it can make the whole dish more vibrant and pleasing to the eye. It is widely available at Indian supermarkets. It will surely enhance your dining experience.

❧ Mango powder

Mango powder is an Indian spice that adds a citrusy flavor to dishes. It is made from dried raw mangoes and is a popular condiment used to make chutneys. It is readily available at Indian supermarkets and has a shelf life of up to a year. Mango powder is low in calories and has anti-inflammatory properties, making it an ideal choice for vegans who avoid dairy products. It is also a good source of vitamin C and aids digestion.

❧ Masoor dal

Masoor dal, also known as red split beans, is easier to cook than other types of beans, and it makes a delicious dal or soup. Its high fiber and protein content means it keeps you fuller for longer. It also supports regular bowel movements and helps prevent constipation. Masoor dal is a perfect choice for those following a vegetarian or vegan diet. The total cooking time is approximately 20 minutes, resulting in a soft, creamy texture.

❧ Mung

Mung beans are a nutritious plant-based protein, full of dietary fiber, vitamins and minerals. They are easy to cook and great for vegetarian and vegan diets. Their fiber content gives them a low glycemic index, making them suitable for diabetics. They help reduce appetite and aid in weight loss. Mung flour is used to make delicious and healthy meals.

❧ Mustard seeds

Mustard seeds are the king of the masala dabba (spice box) and are used in almost every curry and dal dish in India's western and southern regions. It's fun to watch them pop and fizz when they are added to hot oil, but it's important to remember to work quickly; otherwise, the seeds will burn in the hot oil, which can ruin the dish entirely.

❧ Pickle masala

This is a ready-to-use raw masala that can be used to enhance the flavor and look of many dishes including curry and dal. It is readily available at Indian supermarkets. Pickle masala is also known as Achar masala. Fenugreek seeds, its primary ingredient, are known to regulate blood sugar levels and promote a healthy digestive system.

❧ San Marzano tomatoes

Originating from the San Marzano region of Italy, these tomatoes are full of flavor and natural sweetness and have a rich, creamy texture, making them perfect for pasta sauce. If you are a fan of pasta, you must try making a San Marzano tomato sauce. They will help you create a classic and authentic Italian sauce, giving your homemade meal a five-star touch. They can also be used in salads, soups and stews. During the summer, you can easily find them fresh at farmers markets.

❧ Tamarind

Tamarind is a tropical fruit that thrives in hot weather. It has a long and curved shape, is brown in color, and contains seeds. It has a very strong tangy taste that makes it ideal for creating sweet and sour dishes. Tamarind is also very affordable and widely used in cooking, especially in Asia, the Middle East, and Latin America. It is a highly nutritious fruit, rich in minerals, vitamins and dietary fiber, and can help reduce inflammation and promote overall joint health. To make tamarind pulp, see page 48.

❧ Thai Curry Paste

Thai curry paste is readily available at Asian supermarkets and regular grocery stores. It creates a fiery flavor and aroma that makes one drool at the thought. Thai curry paste is one of the most important ingredients in Thai cuisine, and is known for its aromatic, warm and exotic flavor profile.

❧ Tur or toor dal *(split pigeon peas)*

These split peas are commonly used in day-to-day cooking in Gujarat. They offer a good amount of protein and make a flavorful dal. It is no surprise they are one of the most consumed splits in Gujarat and South Indian regions. As a result, Tur has found a permanent place in the Gujarati kitchen.

❧ Turmeric powder

Turmeric offers impressive health benefits and is considered a super spice. It continues to gain popularity due to its incredible medicinal properties. A little spoon can go a long way and bring a bright yellow color to your dish.

Snacks & Light Meals

Blistered Shishito Peppers

When I first laid eyes on those adorable little green peppers in New Mexico, it was love at first bite. Or sight. Or both really; I just fell head over heels.

I highly recommend this recipe if you have access to a local farmer's market. I love to pick my peppers up from our local farmer's market; they are usually top quality and better than anything I can find in the grocery store. It also feels great to support our wonderful and hard-working local farmers.

SERVES 4

1 tbsp olive oil

175g/6¼oz shishito peppers, washed and dried

¼ tsp chili flakes

¼ tsp flaky salt, plus ½ tsp to garnish

Juice of ½ lemon

Heat the olive oil in a wok/frying pan over a medium-high heat. Add the shishito peppers and cook until they are blistered – this takes about 2 minutes, stirring continuously. Turn off the heat and add the chili flakes, salt and lemon juice. Mix well. Garnish with more flaky salt and serve hot as a snack, side dish or appetizer.

Chickpea Waffles with Spinach

If you're on the hunt for an alternative to an egg for your morning meal, waffles made with protein-packed besan (gram/chickpea flour) are an excellent option for you. They make for a flavorful breakfast that will keep you feeling full until lunch. I like to make mine with fenugreek leaves as they really elevate the look and taste, but you can use spinach if that is what's available. You can make this recipe in a waffle maker by simply spreading it on the machine and following the process as you would with regular waffles. Your healthier and fiber-loaded waffles will be ready in a jiffy.

MAKES 4

155g/5½ oz/1¼ cup besan (gram/chickpea flour)

60g/2oz/¼ cup yogurt

2 tbsp oil

175ml/6fl oz/¾ cup warm water

½ tsp ground turmeric

¼ tsp baking powder

35g/1¼oz/½ cup spinach or fenugreek leaves, chopped

1–2 green chilies, shredded

½ tsp garam masala

Mint Chutney with Garlic (see page 159) or Sweet Mango Pickle (see page 150), to serve

In a mixing bowl, combine the flour, yogurt and oil and mix well. Slowly add the warm water and mix until the mixture forms a smooth batter. Add the rest of the ingredients and mix again until the batter is free of lumps.

Heat the waffle maker and pour in 250g/8¾oz/⅓ cup of the batter ensuring the waffle maker is evenly coated with batter. Cook the batter for 2½ minutes, then flip the waffle and cook for another minute. Remove the waffle from the pan. Repeat the process and cook the remaining batter to make 5 waffles, then serve warm with mint chutney or homemade sweet mango pickle.

Biscuit Gujarati Bread
(Biscuit Bhakri)

This wonderfully crispy bread is a popular breakfast bread in Gujarati households, and is also affectionately known as the travel snack. It's made with ghee and sooji (coarse semolina) and comes from the Rajkot district of Gujarat; the region is famous for it. What I love about it is that you can pop it straight into your toaster to heat – enjoy it for breakfast with a steaming cup of masala chai and your day is made. When I shared this recipe with my foodie fans, I received lovely text messages for days.

MAKES 9–10

130g/4¾oz/1 cup wholemeal/whole-wheat flour

100g/3½oz/½ cup coarse semolina (sooji)

4 tbsp ghee, plus 1–2 tbsp extra for spreading on the bread

½ tsp salt

7 tbsp full-fat milk, warmed

Combine the flour, semolina, ghee and salt in a mixing bowl. Add the warm milk and bring the mixture together into a dough, then knead for 5–6 minutes until smooth. The dough should be firm. Let it rest for 15 minutes.

Divide the dough into 9–10 equal portions and shape each into round balls. Next, press each ball of dough flat between your palms, before rolling them into 13–15cm/5–6in discs on a flat surface.

While you are rolling out the dough, set a heavy-based frying pan over a low heat to preheat.

Add 1 tablespoon of the ghee to the preheated pan and add 2–3 discs to the pan. Cook on one side for 4 minutes, pressing with a damp cloth until golden brown spots appear on the underside of the breads. Flip them over and cook the other sides for 3 minutes. Repeat to cook all the bread, adding a little more ghee to the pan each time.

Spread ½ teaspoon of ghee on each bread, and allow the breads to cool before storing in an airtight container for up to a week.

Crispy Lentil Snack
(Jada Mathia)

This is a beloved Diwali snack; you will find it in every Gujarati kitchen. This recipe comes from my elder sister, so it is 100% authentic. This crunchy, golden snack has distinctive sweet and spicy flavors – my husband can feast on them 24/7. It is always in my kitchen, keeping me in touch with my roots.

MAKES 20-25

FOR THE SUGAR WATER
3 tbsp sugar
3 tbsp water

FOR THE MATHIAS
200g/7oz/1¼ cup mathia flour (readily available at Indian supermarkets)
4 tbsp whole-wheat/ wholemeal flour
1 tsp carom seeds (ajwain seeds), slightly crushed
1½ tsp sesame seeds, slightly crushed
1½ tsp chili powder
½ tsp ground turmeric
1¼ tsp salt
4 tbsp oil, divided
500ml/17fl oz/2 cups oil, for deep frying, plus extra to grease your hands

To make the sugar water, heat the water in a small pan and bring to the boil. Add the sugar and stir until it is completely dissolved, then set aside.

Combine all the remaining ingredients and 3 tablespoons of the oil in a mixing bowl and mix well. Slowly add 2 tablespoons of the sugar water and knead the dough. Add the remaining water to make a tight dough. If the dough is dry, add 1–2 teaspoons water. The dough should be smooth. Grease your hands and the dough with 2 teaspoons of oil and knead for 2–3 minutes until soft.

Place two dish towels on a steady surface, such as your kitchen worktop, and place the bowl with the dough on top. Beat the dough with a pestle for 5 minutes to ensure the dough is soft and easy to roll. (If you don't have a pestle, you can use a small, clean hammer, by putting the dough in a stainless-steel bowl and pounding it with the hammer.) Cover the bowl and set aside to rest for 15 minutes.

Divide the dough into 20-25 equal portions and coat with the remaining 1 tbp of oil. Then, shape each portion into a round ball. Press the balls flat between your palms, before rolling them into 3cm/1½in in discs on a flat surface.

Heat the oil in a deep saucepan over a medium heat. It should be hot, but below smoking point. To check the oil is hot enough, take a small piece of dough and drop it into the oil. If the dough rises to the surface immediately, then your oil is ready. Add 2–3 discs to the oil at a time and fry for 5–6 seconds until golden. Flip them over and fry for another 2–3 seconds. Remove the Mathias from the oil with a slotted spoon, and transfer to a plate lined with paper towels to drain.

Spicy Chickpea Crepes
(Besan Chilla or Gujarati Pudla)

The Gujarati *pudla* aka 'puda' is a vegetarian pancake made with gluten-free besan (gram/chickpea flour). Pudla is commonly eaten in Gujarati households and only requires a little kitchen expertise. It is tasty, protein-packed and versatile, making it an excellent option for light suppers, breakfast or afternoon snacks. In addition, it's easy to make – a convenient option after a long day at work.

MAKES 8 CREPES

- 240g/8½oz/2 cups besan (gram/chickpea flour)
- 4 tbsp rice flour
- 2 tbsp coarse semolina (sooji)
- 130g/4½oz/½ cup plain yogurt
- 2–3 tbsp oil
- 600ml/20fl oz/2½ cups warm water
- 2–3 green chilies, finely minced
- 2½ tsp garlic paste
- Large handful of cilantro/coriander, finely chopped
- 1¼ tsp garam masala
- 1 tsp ground turmeric
- 1 tsp ajwain seeds
- 2–3 tsp sugar, optional
- 1¼ tsp salt
- 5–6 tbsp oil, for frying
- Sweet Mango Pickle (see page 150), to serve (optional)

Put the flours, semolina and yogurt in a mixing bowl and stir to combine. Slowly add the oil and the warm water and stir to make a smooth, lump-free batter. Add all the remaining ingredients and mix well until everything is combined, then set aside to rest for 10 minutes. Slowly add up to 5 tablespoons more water if the batter is too thick and mix well.

Heat a non-stick frying pan over a medium-low heat and grease by adding 1 teaspoon of oil. Pour 85ml/3fl oz/⅓ cup of the batter into the pan and use a circular motion to spread the batter out into a thin layer. Fry for 2–2½ minutes until golden underneath, then flip and fry on the other side, adding 1 teaspoon of oil, for a couple of minutes until golden. Transfer to a warm plate or serve hot straight from the pan. Repeat, using the rest of the batter, adding more oil to the pan as needed. Serve with sweet mango pickle.

Karari Roti

Ah, karari roti; I fell in love when I spotted this bread at my favorite restaurant in India, which I visit every time I travel there. It was love at first bite. They are large bowl-shaped crispy roti, welcoming with their lightly golden edges. This recipe is a breeze as it can be made up in a few simple steps. You'll need a kadhai without a handle, or you can use a stainless steel mixing bowl (about 27cm/11in in diameter) as I do.

SERVES 4

125g/4½oz/1 cup plain/
  all-purpose flour, plus extra
  for dusting
¼ tsp salt
2 tbsp butter, melted
5 tbsp warm water, plus extra
  if needed
A little oil, for greasing

TO GARNISH

4–5 tbsp unsalted butter,
  melted
2 tsp chaat masala (readily
  available at Indian
  supermarkets)
1 tsp red chili powder
4 tbsp finely chopped cilantro/
  coriander (optional)

Combine the flour, salt and melted butter in a mixing bowl and mix well. Add the water and bring the ingredients together with your hands to form a ball of dough. Grease your hands with oil and continue kneading for 3–4 minutes until you have a smooth and soft dough. If the dough is dry, add 1–2 tablespoons more water and knead for 1–2 minutes longer. Cover the bowl with a plate and let the dough rest for 15 minutes.

Divide the dough into 2 equal portions and shape each into round balls. Next, press each ball of dough flat between your palms, before rolling them into circles measuring 33–36cm/ 13–14in in diameter.

Turn the kadai or heatproof stainless steel mixing bowl upside down. Lightly grease the surface of the kadai or mixing bowl with 1–2 teaspoons of oil. If you are using an oven, heat the oven to 160ºC/315ºF/Gas 3.

Place a rolled-out disc of dough on the kadai or stainless steel bowl and either bake it in the oven for 15–18 minutes, or on the hob for 8–10 minutes, until light brown spots appear. Once brown spots appear and the dough looks crispy, remove the dough carefully from the kadai or bowl and place it on a large plate to cool down.

Repeat the process to cook the remaining disc.

Add the garnish ingredients to a bowl and mix together. To serve the breads, brush the inside of the cooked roti bowl with the garnish.

Masala Poori
(Turmeric Bread)

Gujaratis tend to bring their food with them while traveling. Whether traveling by plane or train, they will have homemade Masala Pooris or theplas in their bags. If you meet a Gujarati passenger, they will likely offer you a thepla. It is considered impolite not to offer, and equally impolite to refuse. It's a fascinating ritual to observe at 35,000 feet!

Masala Pooris bring back sweet memories for me, as my family used to take them wherever we went. They are convenient travel snacks as they last for a week. Poori are also a popular breakfast item all over India or can be served at lunch or dinner. There is an on-going joke that moms often tell their daughters that they won't be able to find a husband if their roti and poori are not round, since their prospective mother-in-law would test this ability. I have two wonderful daughters who are great cooks. I once told my daughters that if they couldn't make perfect round roti or poori, I had a $7.99 cookie cutter which solved the problem!

MAKES 16

250g/8¾oz/2 cups whole-wheat/wholemeal flour

½ tsp ajwain seeds

½ tsp cumin seeds

1½ tsp chili powder

1 tsp ground turmeric

1½ tsp coriander-cumin powder (see page 20)

5 tbsp oil, plus 500ml/17fl oz/ 2 cups for deep frying

½ tsp salt

125ml/4½fl oz/½ cup warm water

Curry or pickle, to serve

Combine the flour, spices, 3 tablespoons oil and salt in a medium bowl and mix well. Add spinach or fenugreek leaves, if using, then pour in the warm water. Mix well, then knead for 3–4 minutes until you have a smooth and tight dough. Cover the bowl with a plate or cling film/plastic wrap and set aside to rest for 15 minutes.

Once rested, divide the dough into 16 equal portions and shape each into round balls. Next, press each ball of dough flat between your palms, before rolling them into 7½cm/3in discs on a flat surface. If they're too thick or too thin, they won't puff.

Heat the 500ml/17fl oz/2 cups oil in a deep saucepan over a medium heat. Frying temperature should be not be too hot or too cold. Cool oil can prevent pooris from puffing. To test the oil temperature, drop a small piece of dough into the hot oil and if it rises immediately, it is ready. Working in batches, add 2–3 pooris to the oil and fry for 2–3 seconds until lightly golden brown. Flip the pooris and fry the other side for 1–2 seconds. To puff the pooris, gently tap them with the back of a skimmer or frying spoon. Once golden and puffed, use a slotted spoon to transfer the pooris to a plate lined with paper towels to drain. Repeat the process with the remaining dough.

Serve the poori piping hot with your favourite curry or pickle.

Mung Sprout Crêpes

Packed with protein and fibre, healthy mung sprouts can be a great addition to vegan or vegetarian crêpes. Having this mung crêpe for breakfast can help to increase protein intake and reduce carbs – and is sure to lift your spirits and enhance your health.

You will want to plan ahead to make this recipe, and start soaking your mung beans the day before you want to make the crêpes. To soak the mung beans: Rinse the beans, then soak them in 480ml/16fl oz/2 cups water for 24 hours. Reserve the soaking water, which will be used in the recipe.

SERVES 4

200g/7½ oz/1 cup soaked mung beans (see instructions above)

2–3 green chilies, roughly chopped

3 garlic cloves, peeled but left whole

60g/2oz spinach, washed, dried and roughly chopped

2 tsp cumin-coriander powder (see page 20)

1¼ tsp salt

65g/2½oz/½ cup besan (gram/chickpea flour)

3–4 tbsp oil, to cook the crepes

Tomato and Chana Dal Chutney (see page 158) or thecha paste (see page 63), to serve

To make the crêpe batter, combine all the ingredients, except the besan and oil for cooking, in a blender, along with the mung soaking water, and blitz to make a coarse paste. Add the besan to the blender and blend again for 15 seconds, then transfer the batter to a small bowl.

Preheat a non-stick frying pan or crêpe pan over a low heat for 3–5 minutes. Grease the pan with about 1 teaspoon of oil. Scoop up about 85ml/3fl oz/⅓ cup of the batter and pour it into the pan, and use a circular motion to spread it evenly and create a thin layer. Cook for 2½ minutes, then flip the crêpe over and cook on the other side for 1½ minutes until brown spots appear. Transfer the crêpe to a plate and serve hot with tomato and chana dal chutney or thecha paste.

Repeat the process to cook the remaining batter, although any leftover batter can be stored in the refrigerator for up to 4 days.

THE HERBS AND SPICES OF INDIA

Every few years, I return to Gujarat to spend the summer with my family. While there, I make it my mission to learn more recipes from all the women in my family. My family are keen to see more of India, so we began to split half the time with the extended family in Gujarat, and the other half to see different regions of India, expanding my culinary knowledge of India even more.

Each region of India has its own distinct language, culture and architecture, and most noticeable of all is how diverse the cuisine is. Being the forever inquisitive foodie, I picked up interesting recipes whenever I could coax the chef to share their secrets, and when that didn't work, I would come home and reverse-engineer the recipes I loved. My Indian recipes are my gift to you: here is everything I learned as I traveled across vibrant India. I am introducing to you some of the best dishes of regional food and the remarkable diversity that India offers.

I've picked some real crowd-pleasers in this book. If you love to snack, but are looking to avoid fast food, Gujarati snacks are generally healthy and light – unlike other snacks around the globe which tend to be heavy and full of fat. Big on flavor and easy on the grease, the snacks and appetizers within these regions are ideal for those who crave snacks without the junk.

If you venture a little deeper into the regional cuisines of India, you will discover some of the tastiest meals to devour any time of the day, such as Kasuri Methi and Papad Curry, and Semolina Rolls, the fiery seafood and the tangy mouth-watering chaat street foods of Mumbai, vibrant dishes with coconut and curry leaves from the coastal state of Kerala, and a few dozen exotic recipes as well.

I have crafted each recipe to make sure it is simple and easy for even a novice to learn while still retaining the authentic and mouthwatering taste.

Key herbs and spices in Indian cooking:

CUMIN – see Black-eyed Beans in Gravy on page 96, Jeweled EggplantAubergine Chaat on page 95

CILANTRO/CORIANDER – see Butter Paneer Malai on page 116 or Fiery Fish Forever on page 139

TURMERIC – see Masala Poori on page 36, Corn Khichu on page 58 or Spiced Potato Medallions on page 80

CURRY LEAVES – see Andra-style Curry Leaf Chicken on page 132 or Keralan-Style Shrimp/Prawns on page 142

CARDAMOM – Cardamom and Rose Perfumed Baklava on page 166 or Custard-Flavored Fruit Salad on page 168

Sago Balls with Coconut and Curry Leaves
(Sabudana Vada)

These little balls are as much of a feast for the eyes as they are for the taste buds and, whenever I visit a restaurant, they are always the first thing I order off the menu. Unfortunately, not all eateries serve this dish, which is why I recommend you learn to make it. The ingredients are easy to find and usually at hand in your pantry, making these an easy and exciting school lunch item.

The rainy season makes me crave these spicy crunchy balls. The addition of curry leaves and green chilies gives them a wonderfully earthy, rich, and savoury kick that elevates the whole taste experience.

MAKES 10–12

2 medium potatoes

225g/9oz/1½ cup sago (sabudana or tapioca pearls)

4 tbsp roasted peanuts, crushed

8-10 curry leaves, chopped

2 green chilies, finely grated

4cm/1½in piece of fresh root ginger, finely grated

4 tsp lime juice

1 tsp sugar

1½ tsp salt

500ml/17fl oz/2 cups oil, for deep frying and greasing

Yogurt or green chutney, to serve

FOR THE FILLING

50g/1¾oz/½ cup fresh or frozen shredded coconut (thaw if using frozen)

½ tsp sugar

½ tsp lime juice

1 tsp grated fresh root ginger

1 tsp grated chili

2 tbsp golden raisins/sultanas, roughly chopped (optional)

Handful of cilantro/coriander, finely chopped

Combine all the ingredients for the filling in a small bowl, season with salt and mix well, then set aside.

Put the potatoes and 1–1.4 litres/32–48fl oz/4–6 cups water into a medium-sized deep pan over a medium-high heat. Bring to the boil, partially cover the pan and cook for 45 minutes–1 hour till the potatoes are tender. Let them cool, then peel and set aside.

Combine the tapioca with 480ml/16fl oz/2 cup water in a mixing bowl and let soak for 3–4 hours. Drain off the water completely. Keep aside ½ cup of the soaked tapioca. Add the peanuts, curry leaves, boiled potatoes, green chilies, ginger, lime juice, sugar and salt to the remaining soaked tapioca, and mix well with your hands to make a dough. Now add the ½ cup of tapioca you set aside and mix gently.

With greased palms, divide the dough into 10–12 equal portions and shape each into round balls. Next, press each ball of dough flat between your palms, before rolling them into 8cm/3in discs on a flat surface. Place 2 teaspoons of the filling in the centre of the disc. Bring the sides of the disc together and press them to seal, then shape it into an oval-shaped ball. Repeat the process with the rest of the dough and filling.

Heat the oil in a frying pan over a medium-high heat and add 3 balls. Deep-fry for 2–3 minutes, or until light golden brown. Remove the balls with a slotted spoon and drain on a plate lined with paper towels. Repeat until all the balls are cooked.

Sesame Seed Bombs

If you're after an easy and moreish snack, look no further. This recipe was inspired by visits to the funfair with a cousin when I was a college student. I'm usually not a potato fan, but I was astonished by the heavenly flavour of these balls coated with sesame seeds. For years, I experimented with making them and finally found the perfect balance of taste and crunch.

MAKES ABOUT 12

280g/10oz or approximately 2 medium potatoes

1 carrot, peeled and finely grated

1 green chili, finely chopped

¾ tsp garlic paste

½ tsp garam masala

3 tbsp peanuts, slightly crushed

Large handful of cilantro/ coriander, finely chopped

2 tbsp cornstarch/cornflour

¾ tsp salt

500ml/17fl oz/2 cups oil, for deep frying

72g/½ cup sesame seeds, slightly crushed in a pestle and mortar, or you can crush them on a flat surface using a rolling pin

Tamarind chutney (see page 48), to serve

Place the potatoes in a microwave-safe bowl and cook for 8–10 minutes, or until very soft. Remove from the microwave, peel and discard the skins, and mash the flesh in a bowl until smooth.

Add all the remaining ingredients, except the frying oil and sesame seeds, to the bowl with the mashed potatoes and mix everything together until evenly combined.

Heat the frying oil in a deep saucepan over a medium heat. Scoop a 1½ tablespoon portion of the potato mixture and shape into a ball. Repeat with the rest of the potato mixture until you have approximately 12 balls. Quickly dip each in a bowl of water, then roll in crushed sesame seeds to fully coat.

Working in batches so you don't overcrowd the pan, deep-fry the balls for 2–3 minutes, or until golden brown all over. Remove the balls from the pan with a slotted spoon and drain on a plate lined with paper towels. Serve hot with tamarind chutney.

Vegetable Grilled Cheese Sandwich

Forget soggy grilled cheese sandwiches and enjoy these mouth-watering veggie melts, filled with wonderful savoury flavors that can be made without spending too much time in the kitchen.

A friend of mine made this sandwich for me. At first, I didn't understand why in the world the recipe needed all these vegetables and why they would be appealing. But then I tried it, and wow! The taste and texture hooked me in an instant. To be honest, I'm not a fan of every kind of vegetable out there, but with this veggie melt, I just gobble them all up.

SERVES 4

60g/2¼oz spinach, chopped

2 small carrots, peeled and chopped

2 tomatoes, chopped

1 small red onion, chopped

1 small green chili pepper, minced (or 4–6 shishito peppers, chopped)

2–3 tbsp butter

8 slices of bread

140g/5oz/1½ cups shredded mature/sharp Cheddar cheese, plus more if you like extra cheese

¼ tsp salt

¼ tsp black pepper

Combine all the vegetables and chili in a mixing bowl, season with salt and pepper and mix well.

Butter all 8 slices of bread.

Preheat a large heavy-based frying pan over a medium heat and place 2 slices of bread, butter side down, in the pan. Add one-quarter of the Cheddar to each slice and let it slightly melt. Once melted, add one-quarter of the vegetable mixture to each slice. Place another slice of bread on top, butter side up, and press down gently. Cook for 2–3 minutes, then flip the sandwiches carefully and cook on the other sides for 1–2 minutes, or until they are golden brown all over.

Repeat the process to make the remaining sandwiches and serve to your family with love.

Pani Puri
(Crisp Fried Bread with Spicy Water)

Just the mention of the term 'pani puri' is a drool-inducing experience! The sweet, zingy and spicy flavors are exceptionally matched with the crisp, soft and liquid textures. It is a lip-smacking appetizer that is savored by kids, adults, and the elderly alike. The childlike glee of opening the mouth wide and gobbling up a whole pani puri to relish the flavor explosion in the mouth never gets old!.

Interestingly, assembling the pani puri is as fun as eating it! Of course, everyone enjoys customizing it their way. This recipe pairs it with spicy pani, but you could also enjoy it with a few with a sprinkle of chaat masala, a squeeze of lemon, or a drizzle of the sweet and sour tamarind chutney!

SERVES 4

30–32 crisp fried puris (readily available at Indian supermarkets)

FOR THE PANI (OR SPICY WATER)

25 mint leaves

1 tbsp chopped cilantro/ coriander leaves

2 small green chilies or 1 small Thai green chili (use less/ more as per taste preference)

1 tbsp tamarind pulp (you can buy this, or make your own: see recipe opposite)

5 dates, pitted

½ tsp cumin seeds, roasted

5 tsp pani puri masala (readily available at Indian supermarkets)

FOR THE POTATO FILLING

250g/8¾oz potatoes

120g/4¼oz/½ cup black bengal gram/kala chana, dried, or 1 can of garbanzo beans, drained and rinsed

1 small red onion, chopped

1 tsp ground cumin

1 tsp red chili powder

Salt

FOR THE TAMARIND CHUTNEY

YIELD: 1 CUP OF CHUTNEY

170g/6oz/1 cup brown sugar

250ml/8fl oz/1 cup water

140g/5oz/½ cup tamarind pulp

½ tsp salt

½ tsp chili powder

1 tsp cumin seeds, ground

TO MAKE HOMEMADE TAMARIND PULP

YIELD: 510G/18OZ/2 CUPS

1 litres/32fl oz/4 cups water

300g/10½oz tamarind

1 Add the water to a medium-sized deep pan and bring to the boil over a high heat. Add the tamarind and cook for 3–4 minutes. Leave the tamarind and hot water for 1 hour.

2 Using a potato masher or your hands, press the soaked tamarind through a colander to collect the pulp. Transfer the pulp to an airtight container and keep in the refrigerator for up to a week or the freezer for up to 3 months.

RECIPE CONTINUES OVERLEAF

❧ ❧ ❧ ❧ ❧ ❧ ❧ ❧ ❧ ❧ ❧ ❧ ❧ ❧ ❧

To make the pani (spicy water), combine the mint leaves, cilantro leaves, green chilies or Thai green chili, tamarind pulp, dates, cumin seeds, pani puri masala and 500ml/16fl oz/2 cups of water in a blender and blitz to make smooth paste. Strain the water into a bowl and keep in the refrigerator for about 2 hours to bring out the flavours.

To cook the potatoes, put the potatoes and 1–1.4 litres/32–48fl oz/4–6 cups water in a medium-sized deep pan over a medium-high heat. Bring the water to the boil, partially cover the pan and cook for 45 minutes to 1 hour till the potatoes are tender. Let them cool, and then peel and set aside.

If you are using dried black Bengal gram (kala chana), you can cook your beans at the same time. Place the beans in a deep saucepan and cover with 1–1.4 litres/32–48fl oz/4–6 cups of hot water and let it soak for 2 hours. Bring to the boil, skimming off froth as needed. Cover and cook over a medium heat for 1 hour until the beans are very tender. Drain the excess water and leave to cool for 5–7 minutes.

To create the potato filling

Roughly mash the boiled and peeled potatoes in a bowl. Add the cooked black gram, chopped onion, cumin, red chili powder. Season with salt, then mix everything together well and set aside.

To prepare the tamarind chutney

Put the brown sugar in a deep saucepan and add 120ml/4fl oz/½ cup of water. Cook over a medium heat for 5–6 minutes, stirring occasionally, until it reduces down to a sticky syrup that coats the back of the spoon. Whisk in the tamarind pulp until well combined, season with salt, chili powder and ground cumin seeds, then remove the saucepan from the heat. Let the sweet chutney cool completely before using.

To assemble the pani puri, crack a small hole in a crisp fried puri, stuff in some potato filling, and drizzle a bit of tamarind chutney over. Dunk the puri in the pani (spicy water) right before gulping it down in one go.

Leftover tamarind chutney can be stored in a container in the refrigerator for a week or in the freezer for up to 3 months.

Mushroom Soup

This recipe is my take on a mushroom soup that I first tasted while on a trip with my family to the Masa Mara Park in Kenya in 2005. We were hungry when we arrived and went to their restaurant. The head chef came out to take our order. Naturally, I asked to see the menu. He smiled ear to ear and said "Mrs Patel, we don't have menus at Kitchwa Tempo. you and your family can order whatever you like—Indian, Chinese, Thai, Mexican—and we'll prepare it for you." I fell in love with the idea as that's exactly how we eat at home. It felt like stepping into my own kitchen, where I'd whip up a variety of dishes based on everyone's preferences. The absence of a fixed menu and the diverse selection of cuisines put me at ease and made my vacation one of the most memorable. My husband enjoyed his Indian food, my daughter burritos and salsa, my son got his favorite pasta dish, the little Ravina devoured baby food, and myself a nice fish fillet with aromatic spices.

During our time there, the chef served up a delicious spicy mushroom soup, and we all lit up with excitement when we tasted it. Seeing our excitement, the chef taught us how to prepare his dish ourselves. I will never forget this gentleman's kindness, and I love that every time I make this recipe, I am reminded of his incredible hospitality and the way in which he served his food.

SERVES 4

2 tbsp butter

1 onion, roughly chopped

2 garlic cloves, chopped

½ tsp ground coriander

1¼kg/3lb brown mushrooms (such as baby bella/cremini), washed and roughly chopped

1 litres/32fl oz/4 cups broth/ stock, of your choice

Salt, to taste

1 tsp freshly ground black pepper

1 tbsp heavy/double cream

TO SERVE

1 tbsp chives, finely chopped

50g/2oz/½ cup croutons

4 tsp sour cream or heavy/ double cream

Heat the butter until melted in a saucepan. Once melted, sauté the onion for 10 minutes over a medium-low heat.

Add the garlic and ground coriander and cook gently for 5 minutes, stirring continuously.

Add the mushrooms and cook for 5–7 minutes until they have softened. Once soft, add the broth, and season to taste with salt and black pepper. Bring this to a boil.

Remove the pot from the heat and allow to cool. Blend the contents to a smooth consistency. Transfer the soup back to the same pan and bring it to a boil once more.

Mix in the cream and serve the soup hot with some chives, sour cream and croutons.

Steamed Cabbage Snack
(Muthias)

While this dish can work for lunch or dinner, if you're looking for a flavorful and satisfying start to the day, consider giving this Gujarati breakfast a try. If you're used to a bowl of cereal for breakfast, you might be surprised to learn that most commercial cereals are loaded with sugar and are not the healthiest choice. However, there's a delicious and nutritious alternative: muthia. It replaces cereal in our house, as it contains more healthy ingredients and is higher in protein than most cereals, so can help you feel fuller for longer and reduce snacking between meals. It is light and can be enjoyed straight from the steamer with a drizzle of flavoured oil. You can prepare this dish in advance; leftovers can even be frozen and reheated, making it a perfect option for busy weekdays. I may not have appreciated its simplicity as a child, but now this recipe is a staple in my kitchen and has my mouth watering even at the thought.

SERVES 4

2 tsp oil, to grease steamer basket

FOR THE MUTHIAS:

½ green cabbage (approx. 250g/8¾oz) or 2 zucchini, grated

35g/1¼oz/¼ cup whole-wheat/wholemeal flour

50g/1¾oz/¼ cup coarse semolina (sooji)

120g/4¼oz/1 cup besan (gram/chickpea flour)

1 tbsp chili paste

2 tsp ginger paste

¾ tsp ground turmeric

2½ tsp ground coriander-cumin powder (see page 20)

1 tsp salt

2 tbsp yogurt

1 tsp lime juice

¼ tsp baking soda/bicarbonate of soda

1 tsp sugar

2 tbsp oil, plus extra for greasing

FOR THE SEASONED OIL:

3 tbsp oil

2 tsp mustard seeds

½ tsp asafoetida (hing)

1–2 tbsp sesame seeds

RECIPE CONTINUES OVERLEAF

Preheat the steamer and fill it with 1.4 litres/48fl oz/6 cups of water. Grease the steamer tray with oil and place in the steamer.

For the muthias, combine all the ingredients in a large bowl and mix well with your hands to make a dough. Slowly add up to 2 tablespoons more water if needed. With greased palms, divide the dough into 6 equal portions. Take each portion and place on your palm. Make a hole in the middle using a fingertip to give a donut shape.

Place the donuts in the prepared steamer tray and steam over a medium heat for 25–28 minutes, or until an inserted toothpick or fork comes out clean. Carefully remove the steamed muthia from the steamer using tongs or a spatula. Allow the muthia to cool.

For the seasoned oil, heat the oil in a frying pan and add the mustard seeds. When they start to crackle, add the asafoetida and sesame seeds. Mix well and cook for 3–4 seconds. Add the muthia to the pan, stir gently until coated well, and cook for 2-3 minutes until lightly crisp. Serve warm.

Note: For this recipe it's important to wash the entire cabbage before grating it, to prevent the batter from becoming too watery.

Note: If you're not using a steamer, you will need a 20cm/8in baking pan. First, bring 1440ml/48oz/6 cups of water to a simmer in a wok, large frying pan over a medium heat. Place a 5cm/2in steamer rack in the center of the wok and put a greased heatproof or stainless-steel 20cm/8in plate on top (about 5cm/2in deep, traditionally called a thali). Cover it and heat until steam escapes through the lid. Once the water starts boiling, reduce the heat to medium. Remove the lid and arrange the shaped muthia donuts on the steamer basket, leaving enough space between each piece for even steaming. Cover the steamer with its lid to trap the steam. Steam the muthia for about 25–28 minutes, or until fully cooked. You can test for doneness by inserting a toothpick into the center of a muthia, and it should come out clean when it's ready. Once cooked, carefully remove the steamed muthia from the steamer using tongs or a spatula. Allow the muthia to cool.

Samosa Chaat with Fruit
(Traveling Samosas)

We take samosas everywhere we go. In June 2019, my daughter Elissa invited the whole family to celebrate a big day in New York. She was opening a fashion store in the West Village. We would be flying from California to be there. As we were preparing for the trip, I texted Elissa to ask her if I could bring along 60 samosas, a popular and delicious Indian appetizer, for her event. She declined, firmly lecturing me: "Mom, you are traveling 2,500 miles on a plane. You cannot bring sixty samosas with you." I insisted, telling her that I could check them in. She replied: "You cannot check in sixty samosas!!!!" and promptly texted the rest of the family asking that they search my suitcase for samosas before departure.

My son Aamir giggled about this exchange and renamed our family group chat "Traveling Samosas". We instantly fell in love with this name because the phrase truly encapsulates our family and the way we eat, love and live.

Since samosas are famous across the globe, I always wanted to learn how to make authentic samosas, not just any samosas. And was in luck: I first learned how to make Delhi-style samosas from my neighbour's aunt, an amazing cook based in Delhi who insisted on teaching me her dishes. Her samosa recipe is one of the best and has created many amazing dinners for us. When we visited her in March 2023, she welcomed us with homemade samosas, and later that day, we went out for dinner to one of the finest restaurants in New Delhi, but no restaurant could compete with her samosas.

My elder daughter loves samosas with chole, so if you're a fan, try adding one cup of chole on top before adding all the sauces for an extra burst of flavor.

Samosa Fruit Chaat is a delicious refreshing chaat that you can make using good quality store-bought cocktail samosas. However, if you're interested in making homemade samosas, I have included a recipe as well. I was fortunate enough to learn the art of making perfect samosas from a samosa expert chef, and the image of the samosas speaks for itself.

This is a versatile dish that can be shared with a myriad of side dishes and dips. Some examples to get you started include pomegranate seeds, beets, tomatoes, blueberries, or mango chunks.

RECIPE CONTINUES OVERLEAF

MAKES 20–24 SAMOSAS

FOR THE DOUGH

200g/7oz/1½ cups plain/
all-purpose flour

¼ tsp salt

4 tbsp oil

FOR THE FILLING

1½ tbsp oil

1 tsp cumin seeds

Pinch of asafoetida (hing)

35g/1¼oz/¼ cup peas, boiled

280g/10oz or approximately
2 medium potatoes

2 green chilies, finely grated

½ tsp red chili powder

¾ tsp garam masala

2 tsp mango powder (amchur
powder, readily available at
Indian supermarkets)

½ tsp salt

Large handful of cilantro/
coriander, thick stems
removed and leaves chopped

500ml/17fl oz/2 cups oil,
for deep frying

FOR THE SAMOSA CHAAT

1 cup tamarind chutney
(see page 48)

1 cup yogurt sauce
(see page 95)

½ cup mint chutney with Garlic
(see page 159)

1 small red onion, chopped

4–5 tbsp pomegranate seeds
(optional)

60g/2oz/¾ cup sev

4 tbsp chopped cilantro/
coriander

To prepare the dough, mix the flour, salt and oil in a mixing bowl until well combined. Gradually add 5–6 tablespoons of water, until the mixture comes together into a dough. Knead the dough for 2–3 minutes until it becomes soft and smooth. If the dough is too dry, add 1 teaspoon more water and continue to knead. Cover the dough with a plate and set it aside.

To cook the potatoes, put the potatoes in 1–1.4 litres/32–48fl oz/4–6 cups water in a medium-sized deep pan over a medium-high heat and partially cover the pan. Cook for 25–30 minutes until tender. Let them cool, then peel and set aside.

For the filling, heat the oil in a broad frying pan over a medium heat. Add the cumin seeds and, once they crackle, add the asafoetida and peas, and cook for 3 minutes. Add the potatoes, green chilies, chili powder, garam masala, mango powder, salt and cilantro. Mix well and cook for 4–5 minutes until the mixture is well incorporated.

To make the samosas, divide the dough into 20–24 equal portions and shape each into round balls. Next, press each ball of dough flat between your palms, before rolling them into 15cm/6in discs on a flat surface. Cut each disc in half. Take one half and apply water on the straight edge. Now bring the two ends of the straight edge together and roll it into a cone, sealing the edge with water. Fill the cone with 2 tablespoons of the filling and fold in the longer end of the cone, giving the cone structure to stay upright when placed on a flat surface. Use a little more water to seal the edges of the cone, fully enclosing the filling. Repeat the process until all the samosas are made.

Heat the oil for deep-frying in a deep saucepan over a medium heat and carefully lower in 2–3 samosas. Fry for 3–4 minutes, using a slotted spoon to move them around in the oil, until they are golden brown on all sides. Remove the samosas using the slotted spoon or a skimmer and transfer to a plate lined with paper towels to drain. Repeat to cook the remaining samosas.

To assemble the samosa chaat, lay a samosa on a serving plate with the pointy corner facing upwards. Pour one sauce at a time on top of the samosa, making sure to cover it evenly.

Sprinkle red onion, pomegranate seeds, if using, sev and chopped cilantro on top and serve immediately.

Corn Khichu

On my most recent trip to Mumbai, India, I was all set to indulge in the city's finest dining establishments and taste all the upscale dishes I could get my hands on. But my daughter Elissa had other plans and insisted I try this specific dish. I'm so grateful to her for introducing it to me. Despite being a corn skeptic, I was pleasantly surprised and quite intrigued by how much flavor was packed into a simple corn dish! I was so smitten, I returned to the same restaurant to try it again. Determined to bring the taste back home, I put on my culinary cap and experimented a bit. After one or two hiccups, I finally succeeded in replicating that bright golden dish.

SERVES 4

¾ tsp cumin seeds

½ tsp salt

130g/4½oz/1 cup cornflour

110g/3¾oz/½ cup plain yogurt, whisked

2 tsp groundnut (peanut) oil

FOR THE SEASONING:

2 tbsp groundnut (peanut) oil

½ tsp mustard seeds

8–10 curry leaves

½ tsp asafoetida (hing)

2 whole dried red chilies, cut in half

1 tbsp garlic paste

½ tsp ground turmeric

2 tsp Kashmiri red chili powder

1 tsp coriander-cumin powder (see page 20)

TO SERVE:

40g/1½oz/½ cup corn chevda (readily available at Indian supermarkets)

2 tbsp chopped cilantro/coriander

Bring 750ml/26fl oz/3 cups water to the boil in a deep saucepan over a high heat. Add the cumin seeds and salt, then boil for 6 minutes. Turn the heat down to low, add the cornflour to the pan and stir continuously until the batter thickens. Stir in the yogurt and mix well to ensure the batter is free of lumps. Add the oil to the mixture, cover the pan and cook over a low heat for 3–4 minutes. Transfer the corn khichu to a serving bowl.

For the seasoning, heat the oil in a medium-sized pan over a medium heat and add the mustard seeds. When the seeds start to crackle, add the curry leaves, asafoetida, dried chilies and garlic paste. Mix everything and cook for a minute until the garlic turns light brown. Turn the heat off and then add the turmeric, chili powder and the coriander-cumin powder. Stir well, then pour over the khichu and mix.

Garnish with corn chevda and cilantro and serve hot.

Semolina Rolls with Pesto Sauce

I've been making these rolls for as long as I can remember, and I love them. Paired with oh-so-delicious pesto sauce, these rolls are a ray of sunshine for my college kid, who craves them after a long day of studying and eating dorm food. When you are mixing and matching recipes, sometimes you'll envision a fusion of ingredients that go well together – and this is one of those perfect matches.

Try making them a couple of times before expecting to perfect the recipe.

MAKES 22–24 ROLLS

FOR THE ROLLS:
180g/6¼oz/1 cup coarse
  semolina (sooji)
2 tbsp rice flour
120g/4oz/½ cup yogurt
¾ tsp sugar
¾ tsp salt
½ tsp chili flakes
3 tbsp chopped basil leaves

TO GARNISH
5–6 tbsp Vina's Pesto
  (see page 104)
5–6 tbsp olive oil
2 tbsp pine nuts
1 tbsp chopped basil leaves

To make the rolls, combine the semolina, rice flour, yogurt, sugar, salt and 500ml/17fl oz/2 cups water in a bowl and whisk to make a smooth batter. Add the chili flakes and chopped basil leaves and mix well.

You can use an electrical steamer to steam the batter. (If you don't have a steamer, you will need a 20cm/8in greased heatproof baking pan or stainless steel plate that is about 5cm/2in deep – traditionally a thali is used – which will fit comfortably into a wok or large, deep pan. Bring 1.4 litres/48fl oz/6 cups water to a simmer in the wok or pan over a medium heat. Place a 5cm/2in steamer rack in the center of the wok and place the baking pan or plate on top. Cover and heat until steam comes through the lid. Alternatively, you can use a steamer basket attachment if you have one.) Pour 130ml/4½fl oz/½ cup of the batter into the cake pan and steam for 5–6 minutes. Set it aside to cool for 5 minutes, then cut the steamed batter horizontally into 3cm/1½in-wide strips and roll them. Transfer the rolls to a serving plate. Repeat the process with the rest of the batter.

To garnish, combine the pesto sauce with the olive oil. Drizzle the pesto sauce evenly over the rolls and sprinkle with the pine nuts and chopped basil leaves before serving.

Thecha Kachori

I recently went on a trip to Maharashtra with my husband and younger daughter. During a stop at a roadside café, we were served a condiment called thecha paste, which piqued my curiosity. When I couldn't find the exact recipe, I stumbled upon one and decided to try making it. The paste was so delicious that it's now a requested item from my husband who loves these thecha kachoris so much that he'd volunteer to do anything I asked in exchange for some. This recipe is perfect for experiencing an entirely new flavour without having to leave your kitchen.

MAKES 8

200g/7oz/1½ cups plain/
  all-purpose flour

4–5 tbsp oil

½ tsp salt

500ml/17fl oz/2 cups oil,
  for deep-frying

Chutney of your choice,
  to serve

FOR THE THECHA PASTE FILLING

2 tsp oil

8–10 garlic cloves, roughly
  chopped

70g/2½oz/½ cup peanuts

4 green chilies, stems removed
  and cut in half

1 small bunch of cilantro/
  coriander, thick stems
  removed and leaves roughly
  chopped

1½ tbsp sesame seeds

¼ tsp salt

4–5 green chilies, to serve

To prepare the dough, mix the flour, oil and salt in a mixing bowl until well combined. Gradually add 5–6 tablespoons of water until everything is coming together into a dough, then knead for 2–3 minutes until it becomes soft and smooth. If the dough is too dry, slowly add 1–2 teaspoons more water and continue to knead. Cover the dough and set it aside.

Now make the thecha paste. Heat the oil in a broad frying pan, add the garlic and cook for 1 minute, stirring continuously. Add the peanuts and toast for 3 minutes, still stirring. Then add the chilies and cook for 1–2 minutes. Mix in the cilantro and sesame seeds and give it a good stir. Remove from the heat. Once cooled, add the salt and grind the mixture with a mortar and pestle into a coarse paste and set aside.

To make the kachoris, divide the dough into 8 equal portions and shape each into round balls. Next, press each ball of dough flat between your palms, before rolling them into 10cm/4in discs on a flat surface. Spoon one-eighth of the filling paste into the centre of a dough disc. Bring the edges of the dough together to seal the ball, pinching the excess dough from the top together. Press and gently flatten the top. Repeat the process with all the dough and filling to make 8 balls.

Heat the oil for deep-frying in a deep saucepan over a medium heat. Don't overcrowd the pan; lower 2 kachoris into the oil. Fry for 2–3 minutes, using a slotted spoon to move them around, until golden. Using a metal slotted spoon or skimmer, transfer to a plate lined with paper towels. Repeat to cook the remaining kachoris. Serve with your favorite chutney and green chilies.

Salads & Sides

Coconut Rice with Pomegranate

This simple yet picture-perfect dish has a coconutty aroma that makes it satisfying and filling. Not even the highest form of fine dining could dissuade me from indulging in this authentic rice dish when I first saw it. The rice is cooked to perfection, with a little bite to it, garnished with punchy pomegranate seeds and bright green cilantro. The flavor and delivery of this coconutty rice are guaranteed to satiate anyone's rumbling tummy.

Enjoy this simple, satisfying, and visually appealing rice dish on the side of any curry!

SERVES 4

200g/7¼oz/1 cup basmati or
  long-grain rice, uncooked

½ tsp salt

½ tsp cumin seeds

120ml/4fl oz/½ cup canned
  coconut milk

1 tbsp coconut oil, plus extra
  for greasing

TO GARNISH

85g/3oz/½ cup pomegranate
  seeds

A large handful of cilantro/
  coriander, chopped

Rinse the rice once, then put it in a deep pan with 360ml/12fl oz/1½ cups of water, the salt and the cumin seeds, and leave to soak for 30 minutes. After this time, cover the pan with a lid and cook over a medium heat for 10–12 minutes. Add the coconut milk and the coconut oil. Mix gently, and cook for 4–6 minutes over a low heat.

To mold the rice, grease a Bundt cake pan with coconut oil and transfer the cooked rice to it, pressing it down gently. Cover the cake pan with a serving plate and carefully turn it over to turn the rice out onto the plate.

Garnish the top of the rice with pomegranate seeds and cilantro leaves.

Tip: Alternatively, you can use homemade coconut milk. To make it, combine 75g/3oz/1 cup of chopped coconut pieces or grated coconut with 375ml/13fl oz/1½ cups of water in a blender. Blend for 1–2 minutes, then strain and discard the pulp. Leftover milk can be stored in a glass container in the refrigerator for up to 3 days.

Japanese Fried Rice with Mustard Sauce

In my home, Japanese rice with mustard sauce permanently holds a place in our hearts and space in our stomachs. During the pandemic, when we couldn't go out to eat at restaurants, my younger daughter craved Japanese food. This prompted me to seek out Japanese dishes to make at home, and as luck would have it, this one fell into my lap. The pandemic brought much grief, so discovering new recipes was a comfort during this time of uncertainty, which I'm sure many of you also experienced.

SERVES 4

FOR THE GARLIC BUTTER:
4 tbsp melted unsalted butter
1½ tbsp garlic paste

FOR THE RICE:
320g/11½oz/1½ cups sticky or jasmine rice, uncooked
½ tsp salt
3 tbsp groundnut (peanut) oil
1 yellow onion, chopped
1 carrot, peeled and finely chopped
2 eggs, beaten
2 tbsp soy sauce
¼ tsp ground black pepper
1 tbsp sesame oil
2 tsp sesame seeds, toasted, to garnish
1 recipe quantity Creamy Mustard Sauce (see page 69), to serve

Make the garlic butter: combine the butter and garlic in a small bowl, mix well and set aside.

To cook the rice, rinse and then soak in 720ml/24oz/3 cups of water in a medium-sized pan with the salt for 1 hour. Cook the rice along with the soaking water over a medium heat for 15 minutes. Drain the excess water from the rice. Let it cool and leave in the refrigerator for 2 hours to chill.

Heat the groundnut oil in a wok over a medium heat and cook the onion for 4–6 minutes until it is translucent. Add the carrots and cook for another 2 minutes. Push the vegetables to one side of the wok and add the beaten eggs, cooking for 20–30 seconds.

Move the eggs to the side of the pan, add the cooked rice, soy sauce and the garlic butter and cook for a further 2–3 minutes, stirring continuously until all the ingredients are well combined. Season with black pepper and add the sesame oil, and mix well. Garnish by sprinkling the sesame seeds on top.

Serve with creamy mustard sauce.

Note: Leftover rice can be used for this recipe. To avoid food poisoning, it is essential that leftover rice is adequately chilled soon after it is cooked. If in doubt, cook a fresh batch before making the recipe.

Creamy Mustard Sauce

You can't have Japanese rice without mustard sauce. Together they do wonders! The garlic brings out an aroma in the creamy sauce like no other – the flavor just explodes in your mouth.

SERVES 6

3 tbsp mustard powder
180ml/6fl oz/¾ cup soy sauce
1½ tbsp sesame seeds, toasted
½ tsp chopped garlic
4–5 tbsp double/heavy cream

Combine all the ingredients in a blender and blend until smooth.

Transfer the sauce to an airtight glass container and store in the refrigerator for up to 3 days.

Serve with Japanese rice.

Asian-Inspired Red Cabbage Salad with Candied Walnuts

Where I grew up, salad was considered to be weeds (*ghass phoos*) and never made an appearance on the family table. My dad would always reject it, asking why anyone would want to eat it. However, after moving to the United States, I developed a taste for all types of salads and became a complete salad fanatic. My search for new and exciting ingredients to add to my salads continues. That's when I discovered this red cabbage salad, bursting with health benefits. Rau ram, also known as Vietnamese coriander or Vietnamese mint, has a spicy, peppery flavor, which goes so well with this salad. It is available at any Asian store.

SERVES 4

½ red cabbage, approximately 250g/8¾oz, finely shredded

25g/1oz/⅓ cup rau ram (available at Asian supermarkets), thinly chopped

1 small jicama, peeled and cut into matchsticks

20 honey-glazed walnuts or pecans, readily available at supermarkets, or see recipe to make your own

FOR THE DRESSING
3 tbsp lime juice

3 tbsp honey

3 tbsp sesame oil

¼ tsp chili flakes (optional)

½ tsp salt

FOR THE GLAZED PECANS OR WALNUTS
20 walnuts or pecans

2 tsp butter

1 tbsp honey

2 tsp sugar

Pinch of salt

To make the glazed walnuts or pecans: Heat a medium-sized frying pan over a medium heat then add the nuts and roast them for 2 minutes while stirring continuously. Remove the nuts from the pan and keep aside. In the same pan add the butter. Once melted, add the honey, sugar and salt and mix well. Add the roasted nuts back into the pan and continuously stir for 3 minutes until the nuts have caramelized. Transfer the nuts onto parchment paper or a lightly greased plate and let them cool.

To make the dressing, combine all the ingredients in a small bowl and whisk until the sugar is fully dissolved. Season to taste with salt and set aside.

In a large bowl, combine the red cabbage, rau ram, jicama and nuts. Pour over the dressing and mix well. Serve immediately.

Note: It's important to wash the entire cabbage before shredding it, to prevent the salad from becoming watery.

Chickpea and Beet Salad

This quick and easy vegetarian salad is so refreshing. It offers a unique combination of sour and spicy and is packed with flavor. Every time I make this, it goes in a single sitting – with more than half consumed while making it!

SERVES 4

170g/6oz/1 cup dried
  chickpeas/garbanzo beans
2 beets/beetroots
75g/2½oz feta cheese, cubed
4 tbsp lime juice
4 tsp ground cumin
1 tsp chili flakes, to taste
1½ tsp salt

Soak the chickpeas overnight in 1.4 litres/48fl oz/6 cups of cold water. The next day, transfer the chickpeas and their soaking water to a deep pan. Bring to the boil and cook for 45 minutes–1 hour, or until the chickpeas are tender. Drain through a colander and set aside to cool.

You can either boil or roast the beets. To boil, put them into a deep pan with 960ml/24fl oz/4 cups of water. Partially cover the pan with a lid and cook over a high heat for 30–35 minutes until tender.

To roast the beets, preheat the oven to 200ºC/400ºF/Gas 6. Wrap the beets in kitchen foil and bake for 1¼ hours, or until tender when pierced with a knife. Leave to cool and, once cooled, peel the beets and dice them into 5mm/¼in cubes.

To make the salad, combine the cooked chickpeas with all the remaining ingredients, except the beets, in a bowl and mix well. Add the beets last, toss gently, and serve.

Tadka Salad

Ready in five minutes, this colorful cabbage salad makes the most wonderful side dish as it speaks to mindful eating that is tasty and, of course, beautifully presented. I have been eating this perfectly balanced salad for as long as I can remember, and I'm certain that once you've tried it, you will love it as much as I do.

Tadka means tempering spices. Tempering is a crucial part of almost all Gujarati recipes. When tiny mustard seeds are put into hot oil, they begin to sizzle, pop, and bounce all over the pan. The tadka is poured over most dishes as a final step. It adds a nice crunch to every bite you take.

SERVES 4

1½ tbsp oil

1 tsp mustard seeds

Pinch of asafoetida (hing)

40g/1½oz/¼ cup peanuts

2–3 dried chilies

1 green chili, sliced

1 tbsp sesame seeds

½ green cabbage head, approximately 250g/9oz, shredded

5 tbsp pomegranate seeds

10–12 small green grapes

2 Roma or other vine tomatoes, chopped

5–7 yellow cherry tomatoes, sliced (optional)

2 tsp lime juice

¾ tsp salt

For the seasoning, heat the oil in a large shallow pan and add the mustard seeds. Once the mustard seeds begin to crackle, add the asafoetida, peanuts, dried chilies, green chili and sesame seeds. Mix everything well and cook for 3 minutes.

Remove the pan from the heat and add the cabbage, pomegranate seeds, grapes, tomatoes and yellow tomatoes, if using. Add the lime juice and season it all well with salt. Mix well before serving.

Note: It's important to wash the entire cabbage before shredding it, to prevent the salad from becoming watery.

Beet, Feta and Macadamia Salad

This beautiful beet-covered salad evokes excitement and curiosity when tasted for the first time. The colorful combination of ingredients offers a unique taste and look that is irresistible. So why not try it today?

SERVES 4

4 golden or red beets/
  beetroots, thinly sliced

120g/4oz feta cheese, cubed

1 ripe mango, cut into
  ½cm/¼in dice

4 tbsp macadamia nuts,
  roasted

FOR THE DRESSING

3 tbsp extra virgin olive oil

2 tbsp honey or sugar

2 tbsp red wine vinegar

Pinch of ground black pepper

Salt, to taste

Boil the beets (see page 171) and let them cool down. Once cooled, peel and slice into thin medallions and set aside.

In the meantime, make the dressing. In a small bowl, whisk together the olive oil, honey or sugar, red wine vinegar, ground black pepper and salt. Set aside.

In a separate bowl, combine the feta, diced mango and roasted macadamia nuts. Drizzle 3-4 tablespoons of the dressing over the salad and toss well.

Divide the salad equally between 4 plates. Arrange a beet medallion on top of each portion of salad, then overlap more slices around it.

Serve immediately.

THE HERBS AND SPICES OF MEXICO

Mexico is our family's favorite destination to visit. We have been there nearly a dozen times, and each time we return home a few pounds heavier and with a few more unique recipes.

On our first trip to Mexico in 1991, I was underwhelmed by Mexican cuisine. While my family loved Mexican food, it took me a long time to warm up to it. I was not at all impressed with the smell, taste, or look of the food. In a somewhat bizarre turn of events, fast-forward to 2009 and I found myself fully in love with Mexican food. Perhaps my palate and sense of adventure had evolved over those 18 years.

My mind was changed was on a trip to Puerto Vallarta, where we were fortunate enough to rent a villa complete with full-time staff and a chef. The chef sourced fresh ingredients from a local store and prepared everything from scratch. She didn't speak a word of English and I didn't speak a word of Spanish. Her food was over-the-top delicious. After every meal, I would sneak into the kitchen and, through sign language, get the recipe from her. The house manager who spoke English would come in and see us both in action, and he'd step in with a smile and help translate to make sure the recipes were written down correctly. This was a daily routine for the five wonderful days we spent in the villa.

Now enchilada sauce and refried beans have become a part of my cuisine. My fondest recipe from this trip was the enchilada sauce that the lovely chef taught me. I simply love Mexican food now, and I continue to learn more about the fabulous cuisine of Mexico. Much like India, it's a large country with diverse cuisine.

We had a similar experience when visiting Cabo San Lucas in 2017 for the third time. At the end of the trip, the staff snuck a bag full of local spices and ingredients into my suitcase. Saying goodbye to them was like saying goodbye to my family every time I leave Gujarat. They were so kind and warm. What a delightful surprise awaited me when I discovered the groceries on my return home when I unpacked my suitcase! Interestingly, my family in India does the same thing. The tradition of Traveling Samosas continues!

Key herbs and spices in Mexican cooking:

🌿 **CHILI** – see Indian-Style Fusion Pinto Beans on page 79 or Chilaquiles on page 108

🌿 **OREGANO** – see Bean and Cheese Enchiladas on page 122 or Mushroom and Onion Tacos on page 115

🌿 **CILANTRO/CORIANDER** – see Salmon with Chipotle Sauce on page 140

Home-Style Refried Beans

Why settle for canned beans when you can create authentic flavor with this simple recipe?

SERVES 4

200g/7oz/1½ cup dried pinto beans
¾ tsp salt
2 tbsp olive oil
1 tbsp minced garlic
1 yellow onion, finely chopped

Rinse the beans and transfer them to a deep pan with 960ml/32fl oz/4 cups of water. Add the salt and cook over a medium-high heat, partially covered with a lid, for 1½ hours until the beans are very soft and mushy. Remove from heat, drain the excess water, and let them cool. Using a potato masher, mash until creamy.

Heat the oil in a medium pan and sauté the garlic until it turns light brown. Add the onion and cook for 5–6 minutes until soft. Add the cooked beans, with a pinch of salt if needed, and cook over a low heat for 4–5 minutes to warm through. If the beans are too dry, add a splash of water. Serve as a side dish.

Create an amazing Tortilla Cup Salad
Fold 4 tortillas into bowl shapes in a cupcake tin and bake for 10–12 minutes. Fill the cups with Home-Style Refried Beans, plus 2 small chopped tomatoes, 1 small chopped onion, 10 black olive slices, 10 pickled jalapeno slices, ½ iceberg lettuce or Brussels sprouts grated, 120g/4oz grated Cheddar cheese and a sprinkling of sliced scallions/spring onions to garnish.

Indian-Style Fusion Pinto Beans

I've called this bean dish "Indian-style" because in Indian cooking when making dal or beans, we typically sauté onions, garlic, chili and tomatoes in oil. Here I've applied this technique to pinto beans, which are commonly found in Mexican cooking – giving this a fusion twist.

My daughter's friend's mom originally shared with me a recipe for Indian-style pinto beans. With her guidance over the phone, I made it and it turned out great. She later forgot her own recipe, but luckily I had kept it safe and could return it to her, and now to you.

SERVES 4

2 tbsp olive oil
1 tbsp minced garlic
1 yellow onion, chopped
1–2 serrano chili peppers, finely chopped
2 tomatoes, chopped
2 tbsp taco or burrito seasoning
1 × 400g/14oz can of refried pinto beans

Heat the oil in a frying pan over a medium heat. Add the garlic and fry for a minute until golden. Add the onions and chilies and cook for another 6–7 minutes until soft.

Add the tomatoes and cook for 4–5 minutes. Stir in the seasoning and continue cooking for 3–4 minutes. Add the beans and cook for 5–7 minutes until they are well incorporated. Add a splash of water if dry. Serve as a side dish.

Spiced Potato Medallions

Say goodbye to boring French fries – this is an excellent potato alternative. My mom made this potato curry dish for me and my brother when we were kids, and we loved it so much we ate it straight from the pan. Every time I make it now, I think of my brother, who I miss so much. He passed away too soon but left me with many wonderful memories. I dedicate this recipe to him.

SERVES: 4

4 tbsp oil

2½ tsp mustard seeds

½ tsp asafoetida (hing)

4 medium potatoes (approximately 600g/21oz), very finely sliced, ideally on a mandolin

1 tsp ground turmeric

2 tsp red chili powder

3 tsp coriander-cumin powder (see page 20)

½ tsp salt

1 tsp sugar

Heat the oil in a large heavy-based frying pan with a lid over a medium heat. Add the mustard seeds and once they start to crackle, stir in the asafoetida.

Add the potatoes and turn them to coat fully in the oil, then add the turmeric, chili powder, coriander-cumin powder and salt. Stir gently to prevent the slices sticking to each other, ensuring that they are evenly spread in the pan.

Cover the pan and cook for 12–14 minutes until the potatoes are tender. Give them gentle stir every now and then to ensure they're not sticking to the bottom.

Remove from the heat and season with the sugar, stirring gently so the potato slices don't break. Serve hot.

Burrata Salad with Nectarine, Fennel and Kumato

My husband is crazy about this summery salad, and once upon a time, I would make it at least three times a week. It's such an unusual trio of nectarine, fennel and tomatoes – who would've guessed it would make such a perfect combination for a salad? Kumato tomatoes are a dark (almost black) variety of heirloom tomatoes, and they work perfectly with this dish. If you can't find them, a good substitute are other heirloom varieties, or very red and ripe baby plum or cherry tomatoes.

SERVES 4

5 ripe nectarines

1 small fennel bulb, finely sliced

8–10 small Kumato (or other heirloom or baby plum or cherry) tomatoes, sliced

2 balls of burrata cheese (preferably aged burrata)

FOR THE DRESSING

60g/2¼oz basil leaves

4 tbsp good-quality olive oil

4 tbsp balsamic vinegar, aged if possible

2 tbsp brown sugar, honey or agave syrup

½ tsp ground black pepper

½ tsp salt

To make the dressing, combine all the ingredients in a blender or food processor and blitz to a rough consistency.

To assemble the salad, layer up the ingredients on a fancy serving plate starting with the nectarines, followed by the sliced fennel, and topped with the Kumato tomato slices. Place the burrata on top and drizzle the dressing over before serving.

Papaya Salad

This salad is a celebration of Thai flavors. As someone of Gujarati descent, I have a talent for balancing sweet and sour flavors in my cooking. My first attempt at making papaya salad was a success thanks to this skill. Any salad can be enjoyed when the sweet and sour flavors are in harmony, and this recipe is satisfying and delicious. My family loved it so much that I made it three times in one day!

SERVES 4

1 green papaya (approximately 320g/11¼oz) peeled, deseeded and grated

2 juicy tomatoes (approximately 40g/1½oz), sliced into thin wedges

40g/1½oz/¼ cup roasted peanuts, roughly chopped, or 12 cashew nuts, roasted

FOR THE DRESSING:

1½ tbsp sugar (preferably brown sugar)

1 tbsp lime juice (preferably key lime)

1½ tsp garlic paste

1 small Thai green chili, minced

¾ tsp salt

To make the salad dressing, whisk together the ingredients in a small bowl until the sugar is completely dissolved. Set aside.

To assemble the salad, combine the shredded papaya and tomato in a large bowl, crushing the tomatoes slightly with your hands as you add them. Mix well to combine, then pour the dressing over the mixture and toss to coat evenly.

Set aside for 10–15 minutes until the juices from the tomato and papaya have released. Top with roasted peanuts or cashews, and serve immediately.

Roasted Quinoa Salad

I am excited to share this visually appealing and incredibly delicious recipe with all salad lovers! I have expressed my love through food all my life, and finding a unique recipe is one of my favourite things to do. I just cannot wait for you to try this one. Quinoa works so well in a salad, as it keeps you fuller for longer. Roasting it brings out its nutty flavor and adds texture to every bite, making it the perfect base. The aroma of freshly roasted quinoa fills your kitchen and creates a delightful atmosphere. I have also provided a recipe for my Date and Cashew Dressing, which is perfect for those on a vegan diet. It is a great dressing to have in your repertoire because it has a unique combination of sweet and sour flavors along with a nutty and creamy texture. The recipe given below makes more than you'll need for this salad; any extra can be stored in an airtight container in the refrigerator for up to a week.

SERVES 4

2 beets/beetroots

2 tbsp quinoa, uncooked, for roasting

300g/10¾oz/1½ cups quinoa, cooked

1 orange, peeled and chopped

1 celery stalk, finely sliced

6 tbsp Date and Cashew Dressing

FOR THE DRESSING:

8 dates, pitted

4 tbsp lime juice

4 tbsp oil

8-10 cashew nuts

¼ tsp ground black pepper

Salt, to taste

4 tbsp roasted pecan, roughly chopped, to garnish

To cook the beets, preheat the oven to 200ºC/400ºF/Gas 6. Wrap the beets in kitchen foil and bake for 1¼ hours, or until tender when pierced with a knife. Leave to cool and, once cooled, peel and dice them into 1cm/1in cubes.

To make the dressing, combine all the ingredients in a food processor and blend them to a coarse consistency.

To make the roasted quinoa, heat a frying pan over a medium heat and add the 2 tablespoons of quinoa. Roast for 6–8 minutes, stirring constantly. Remove the pan from the heat and set aside.

Combine all the remaining ingredients for the salad in a mixing bowl and mix in the dressing.

To mold the mixture, choose a cup or bowl of your preference (that will fit all the salad in) and fill it to the top with the quinoa mixture. Press it down firmly, then turn out onto a serving plate. Sprinkle the roasted quinoa around the salad and the roasted pecans on top, and serve immediately.

Warm Kale Salad with Golden Garlic

This green salad is easy on the stomach and packed with flavor in every bite. It is the perfect accompaniment to a heavy meal, or a tasty alternative to a bag of chips for those who try to stay away from junk food. Without a doubt, your stomach will thank you.

SERVES 4

2 tbsp groundnut (peanut) oil

8 large garlic cloves, thinly sliced

1 large bunch of kale, washed, deveined and cut into large pieces

120ml/4fl oz/½ cup chicken or vegetable broth

Salt, to taste

¼ tsp ground white pepper

Heat the oil in large, broad frying pan or wok over a medium heat. Add the garlic and cook until light golden brown.

Add the kale leaves and stir-fry with the garlic until the leaves have started to wilt. Add the broth and stir-fry for 1–2 minutes until the leaves have wilted. Add a pinch of salt if needed.

Season with pepper and serve warm before the leaves become soggy.

Tawa Naan with Pesto Sauce

Whenever someone compliments me on being a creative and skilled cook, I tell them I have my foodies – including our 100lb golden retriever, Sir Richard Parker – at home to thank for my success. I discovered this delicious homemade naan recipe on a day when my youngest daughter was craving naan. These fluffy, pillow-like naan are topped with homemade pesto, resulting in an eye-pleasing combination, bridging wonderful flavors from India and Italy. This recipe also can be used to make homemade naan without the tandoor.

SERVES 4

1 tbsp olive oil, plus 2 tbsp for the dough

8 garlic cloves, sliced

230g/8oz/1½ cups plain/ all-purpose flour, plus 4–5 tbsp extra for dusting

½ tsp baking powder

¼ tsp baking soda/ bicarbonate of soda

1 tsp salt

1 tsp sugar

110g/3¼oz/½ cup plain yogurt

3 tbsp warm water

6 tbsp Vina's Pesto (see page 104)

280g/10oz mozzarella cheese, shredded

Heat the oil in a small pan over a medium heat and caramelize the garlic slices until light golden brown. Remove the garlic from the oil and transfer to a small plate.

To make the dough, sift the flour, baking powder, baking soda, salt and sugar into a bowl. Add the 2 tablespoons of oil, the yogurt and the water, and knead for 2–3 minutes until the dough is smooth and soft. Cover with cling film/plastic wrap and let it rest for 15 minutes.

Divide the dough into 4 equal portions and shape each into round balls. Next, press each ball of dough flat between your palms, before rolling them into 20cm/8in discs on a flat surface.

Heat a heavy iron frying pan over a low heat for 4–6 minutes. Coat one side of one of the breads with 2 teaspoons of water so it sticks to the pan, then place it, wet-side down, in the heated pan. Increase the heat to medium-high and cook for 1–2 minutes until bubbles form on top. Using an oven glove/ mitten, flip the pan with naan attached and cook the top side of the bread directly on the flame until brown spots appear.

Spread the naan with 1½ tablespoons of the pesto sauce, then top with 70g/2½oz of the mozzarella and a quarter of the garlic slices. Transfer the topped bread to the same pan and cook for 3–5 minutes until the cheese is slightly melted. Repeat the process with the remaining 3 dough balls.

Serve before it gets soggy.

Vegetarian Mains

Jeweled Eggplant/Aubergine Chaat

Chaat literally means "delicacy"! There is no one, definitive chaat recipe, but my favorite amongst all these tasty small plates is undoubtedly the eggplant chaat. I first tasted this delicacy years ago when I went out to dine at a fancy restaurant with family and friends. I couldn't believe it. Dear Readers, please allow me to paint a picture for you: close your eyes and taste crispy eggplant strips tossed with inviting spices, just a touch of heat, and a creamy and beautifully sweet cumin-flavored yogurt sauce. Try it for yourself!

SERVES 4

FOR THE YOGURT SAUCE
135g/4¾oz/½ cup full-fat yogurt
2¾ tsp sugar
¾ tsp ground cumin
2 tsp water
¼ tsp salt

FOR THE EGGPLANT/AUBERGINES
2 long and thin eggplant/
   aubergines, thinly sliced
   into 16 slices
½ tsp salt
45g/1½oz/¼ cup rice flour
35g/1¼oz/¼ cup besan
   (gram/chickpea flour)
2 tbsp cornstarch
½ tsp chili powder
Pinch of ground turmeric
½ tsp ground coriander
120ml/4fl oz/½ cup water
500ml/17fl oz/2 cups oil,
   for deep-frying

TO SERVE
Tamarind chutney (see page 48)
½ small onion, finely chopped
2 small tomatoes, finely diced
4–5 tbsp sev (readily available
   at Indian supermarkets)
60g/2oz/⅓ cup pomegranate
   seeds

Make the yogurt sauce by combining all the ingredients in a bowl and set aside.

Put the eggplant slices in a bowl and sprinkle with ¼ teaspoon salt. Leave for 30 minutes.

Transfer the eggplant to a colander and rinse with cold water, then dry with paper towels or a clean tea towel/dish towel.

Combine the rice flour, besan, cornflour, chili powder, ground turmeric, ground coriander and ¼ teaspoon salt in a medium bowl. Add the water and mix well to ensure the batter is free of lumps.

Heat the oil in a deep saucepan over a medium heat. Working in batches so you don't overcrowd the pan, coat a few of the eggplant slices in the batter, shake off the excess batter, then drop gently 2–3 slices at a time into the hot oil. Cook for 1–2 minutes, until light golden, then remove with a slotted spoon and leave to drain on a plate lined with paper towels. Repeat to cook the rest of the eggplant slices.

To assemble the chaat, transfer the eggplant slices to a serving plate and drizzle over with yogurt sauce and sweet tamarind chutney. Sprinkle with chopped onion, tomatoes, sev and pomegranate and serve immediately before the eggplant gets soggy.

Black Eyed Beans in Gravy

During the pandemic, my elder daughter's friend, who is like a daughter to me, was unable to return home. She was craving her mother's curry and asked if I could make something similar. I spent a lot of time searching for the perfect dish, but I didn't want to rely on just any online recipe. Instead, I reached out to friends and family to help me find the perfect one. Eventually, I found a recipe that she loved and I was very pleased when she exclaimed, "Aunty, this curry looks exactly like how my mom makes it!" This dish is dedicated to her.

SERVES 4

165g/5¾oz/1 cup dried black-eyed beans

3 tbsp oil

1 tsp cumin seeds

1 tbsp chopped garlic

1 red onion, chopped

2.5cm/1in piece of fresh root ginger, minced

2 tomatoes, chopped

2 tsp coriander-cumin powder (see page 20)

½ tsp ground turmeric

1½ tsp Kashmiri chili powder

1 tsp salt

Handful of cilantro/coriander, chopped, to garnish (optional)

Chapati or rice, to serve

Rinse the beans, then put them in a deep saucepan and cover with 700ml/23½fl oz/3 cups of hot water. Leave to soak for 6–8 hours, or overnight. Discard the soaking water, rinse the beans and add 2 litres/70fl oz/8½ cups of fresh water. Bring the beans to the boil. Remove as much froth as possible from the surface, then partially cover with a lid and cook over a high heat for 1 hour, or until the beans are very tender. Slowly add 475ml/16fl oz/2 cups of water more, if needed, to achieve a mushy consistency. Discard the excess water from the beans.

Heat the oil in a separate pan over a medium-low heat and add the cumin seeds. Once the seeds crackle, add the garlic and cook for 1 minute, then add the onion and ginger and cook for 5–6 minutes until the onion has softened. Add the tomatoes, coriander-cumin powder, turmeric and Kashmiri chili, and season with salt. Mix well and cook for 3–4 minutes until aromatic. Add the beans and 700ml/23½fl oz/3 cups of fresh water to the mixture. Use the back of a spoon to mash a portion of the mixture and simmer for 8–10 minutes until a creamy consistency is achieved. Garnish with cilantro, if using, and serve warm with chapati or rice.

Easy Marinara Pasta Sauce

Looking to make delicious pasta like they do in Italy? I discovered the secret to creating delicious Italian-style pasta with vine-ripened tomatoes 33 years ago, and this recipe has since become a staple in my kitchen.

My husband is in charge of making the sauce, and he has slightly modified the recipe to our liking. I love this "man-made" marinara sauce with my favorite pasta when I need a break from cooking.

SERVES 4

4 tbsp olive oil

2 tbsp chopped garlic

½ tsp chili flakes

½ tsp dried oregano

½ tbsp chopped fresh or
   dried parsley

800g/1¾lb canned Marzano
   tomatoes, 760g/1lb 11oz
   vine-ripened tomatoes
   or Marzano tomatoes

2 tbsp unsalted butter

1½ tsp salt

8–10 basil leaves, roughly
   chopped, plus extra to
   garnish

340g/12oz your choice
   of pasta

25g/1oz/¼ cup shredded
   Parmesan cheese, to serve

Heat the olive oil in a pan over a medium heat and add the chopped garlic. Cook the garlic until caramelized, then add the chili flakes, oregano and parsley. Mix well and cook for 10 seconds.

Add the tomatoes, cover the pan with a lid and cook over a medium-low heat for 8–10 minutes. By now, the tomato skins should be falling off if using fresh tomatoes; remove the skins as much as possible using tongs. If using canned tomatoes, skip this step. Mash the tomatoes using a masher to achieve a chunky consistency. Cook for 5 more minutes.

Add the butter, salt and basil leaves and mix well.

Meanwhile, cook your favorite pasta in a saucepan according to the package instructions and drain.

Serve the pasta and sauce with shredded Parmesan and garnish with basil leaves.

The One & Only Creamy Sauce with Pasta

Once you have created your homemade marinara, you can take it one step further to make the One & Only Creamy Sauce. This sauce has a delicious aroma that wafts through the kitchen, making even the fullest stomachs hungry for a taste. With so few ingredients and such a simple method, this is the ideal way to feed a family for days. I highly recommend trying this sauce with rigatoni.

SERVES 4

1 quantity of Easy Marinara
  Pasta Sauce (see page 100)
4–5 tbsp heavy/double cream
340g/12oz rigatoni pasta
5–6 basil leaves
5–6 tbsp shredded Parmesan
  cheese

Sieve the tomato sauce through a colander into a medium-sized saucepan. Add the cream and cook over a medium-low heat, stirring occasionally, until the sauce thickens. This will take about 3–4 minutes.

In the meantime, cook the rigatoni according to the package instructions and drain.

Add the rigatoni to the sauce and mix well. Divide the pasta between 4 plates and top with basil leaves.

Served hot, sprinkled with Parmesan.

THE HERBS AND SPICES OF ITALY

I've had the pleasure of experiencing delicious gourmet Italian food on multiple trips to Italy. The beautiful alleys of Rome and Florence, Venice, Capri, Anacapri and the Amalfi coast always leave a special and memorable impression on me. Sometimes, I'll spend hours at a random restaurant or coffee shop just to admire the small alleys. One particularly memorable food moment for me was when I tried the perfect marinara sauce at a restaurant near the Rialto bridge in Venice. I hope the Italy-inspired recipes such as my Lemon Butter Sauce with Pasta (see page 125) or Shaved Zucchini Pasta with Pine Nuts (see page 105) transport you to the colorful streets, bustling markets, narrow alleys, and busy kitchens of Italy, and invite you to embrace the rich heritage and culinary delights of this extraordinary country.

My son Aamir fell in love with Italian food on our very first trip to Italy in 1997. On our return, that's all he wanted – he was crazy over it – but when I gave him store-bought marinara sauce he didn't want to take a second bite! So, I had to learn how to make fresh marinara sauce. Needless to say, he grew up on pasta.

With Italian cookery, I've learned the importance of fresh ingredients, such as San Marzano tomatoes, or any vine-ripe tomatoes, basil, parsley, rosemary and chili flakes. Whenever you can, try to find fresh herbs when cooking Italian food.

The key ingredient is using San Marzano tomatoes. I've tried so hard to grow them in my garden, but I lack the "green thumb". When they do grow, the squirrels in my backyard get to them before I can pick them. I always look for San Marzano tomatoes wherever I go, as they are hard to find fresh. If I can't get my hands on fresh, I have half a dozen cans of San Marzano tomatoes on hand in the pantry. I recommend stocking up if you find them too.

I've spent a lot of time finding the best recipes and simplifying them, reducing the number of ingredients while maintaining the rich flavors. The Italian recipes in this book are my family's favorites!

Key herbs and spices in Italian cooking:

𝕃 **BASIL** – see Vina's Pesto on page 104, Semolina Rolls on page 61, Burrata Salad with Nectarine, Fennel and Kumato on page 82

𝕃 **PARSLEY** – see Easy Marinara Pasta Sauce on page 100

𝕃 **OREGANO** – see Vegetable Ragu Pasta on page 107

𝕃 **GARLIC** – See Shrimp/Prawn Penne with Basil, Garlic and Oyster Sauce on page 141 and Warm Kale Salad with Golden Garlic on page 88

Vina's Pesto

This darling green sauce has often come in handy for last-minute lunch and dinner ideas. If, like me, you don't enjoy store-bought pesto sauce, this is the recipe I have perfected at home.

If you're lucky enough to have a garden, the secret to an especially good pesto lies in the use of fresh garlic leaves. Growing your own vegetables and herbs is an excellent way to experience freshness. If you do not have access to fresh garlic, this recipe also works with classic garlic cloves.

YIELD: 250G/9OZ/1 CUP PESTO

2 large bunches of basil leaves (approximately 114g/4oz)

3 large garlic cloves

5g/¼oz/¼ cup fresh garlic leaves, chopped (optional)

2 tbsp pine nuts, or 10 cashew nuts

28g/1oz/¼ cup Parmesan cheese, in chunks

¼ tsp freshly ground black pepper

½ tsp salt

5 tbsp good-quality olive oil

Bring 700ml/25fl oz/3 cups of water to the boil in a deep pan. Turn the heat off and add the basil leaves to the hot water and mix. Leave for 20–30 seconds, using the spoon to stir the leaves and prevent them from turning too dark. Working quickly, remove the leaves from the water and set aside. Let them cool down for 2 minutes.

Combine all the ingredients, except the salt and olive oil, including the basil, in a food processor and blitz for 1½ minutes to a coarse consistency, stopping to scrape down the sides occasionally. Add the salt and 3 tbsp of the olive oil and blitz for another 15 seconds.

Transfer to an airtight container, adding the remaining 2 tablespoons of oil on top, and refrigerate for a week or freeze for up to 1 month.

Shaved Zucchini Pasta with Pine Nuts

If you adore pasta dishes, then this recipe is a show-stopper bursting with health and character. I typically cook it with quinoa spaghetti, but feel free to use your favorite type of pasta. The ripest tomatoes are a must, as they're crucial to the flavor of the dish. This is a light recipe with a generous amount of shaved zucchini, making it an irresistible combination of herbs, nuts and vegetables.

SERVES 4

2 tbsp olive oil

4 tsp finely chopped garlic

2 zucchini/courgettes, trimmed and thinly shaved with a vegetable peeler or on a mandolin

2 tbsp pine nuts

1 tsp chili flakes

1 large handful of spinach leaves, roughly chopped

6 tbsp Vina's Pesto (see page 104)

220g/8½oz angel hair spaghetti, cooked for 1 minute less than package instructions

200g/7oz/1 cup ripe tomatoes, seeds removed, cut into wedges

Salt, to taste

Handful of basil leaves, roughly chopped

6 tbsp shredded Parmesan cheese, to serve

Heat the oil in a wok on medium low heat and add garlic. Cook gently until pale gold, but be careful not to let it burn. Add the zucchini and cook for 2 minutes.

Add the pine nuts and chili flakes and fry for 1 minute. Add the spinach, mix well and cook for 15 seconds. Turn the heat off, add the pesto sauce and mix well.

Transfer the cooked pasta to the pan with the zucchini and stir. Add the tomatoes and salt, then gently stir to combine. Garnish with basil leaves and Parmesan, and serve immediately.

Vegetable Ragu Pasta

Who would have thought that one of my favorite marinara sauces could be found in Costa Rica? I had the pleasure of meeting the co-owners of an Italian restaurant during my visit to Costa Rica. They were both very friendly and welcoming, and they were happy to share with me their secret recipe.

My younger daughter Ravina often requests this sauce because she enjoys it with bucatini. This experience made me realize once again that food can connect people no matter where they come from.

SERVES 6

5 tbsp good-quality olive oil

2 tbsp minced garlic

1 small yellow onion, diced

1 bay leaf

1 tsp chili flakes

1 carrot, peeled and finely chopped

1 large celery stalk, finely chopped

1 tsp dried oregano

3 tbsp chopped parsley leaves

½ tsp ground black pepper

Salt, to taste

800g/28oz canned tomatoes, or fresh Marzano tomatoes are best if you can find them

10–12 basil leaves, plus extra to garnish

Heat the oil in a deep saucepan over a medium heat. Once the oil is hot, add the garlic and cook for 1-2 minutes until it becomes lightly caramelized.

Next, add the onion and bay leaf and cook for 6-7 minutes until the onion becomes translucent.

Add the remaining ingredients, except for the tomatoes and basil leaves, and let it all cook over a medium-low heat for 5 minutes, stirring occasionally. Then add the tomatoes and basil and continue to cook for an additional 15 minutes, stirring occasionally. To achieve a smoother consistency, use a potato masher to break down the chunks.

Garnish with the extra basil leaves and serve it with your favorite pasta.

The leftover sauce can be transferred to an airtight glass container and stored in the refrigerator for a week.

Chilaquiles

I am passionate about trying different restaurants and discovering new recipes, especially while traveling. During a trip to the Midwest, I went out to a recommended restaurant and saw chilaquiles on the menu. I was excited to try the classic spicy dish, but it was a letdown – just a few bland chips topped with chopped bell peppers and strange store-bought salsa. This experience only fueled my passion to experiment and find the perfect chilaquiles recipe. It was eventually taught to me by a grandma chef I met in Mexico, who had a big smile on her face throughout the lesson. After eating hers, I don't think I can try any other.

SERVES 4

1 large black or red dried Mexican chili, left whole

900g/2lb ripe Roma tomatoes

2 green chilies, whole, stems removed

3 large garlic cloves, peeled but left whole

2 stock cubes

Salt, to taste

3 tbsp olive oil

8–10 corn tortillas, cut into 5mm/¼in wide strips

500ml/17fl oz/2 cups oil, for frying

TO SERVE:

125ml/4fl oz/½ cup sour cream, whisked

½ yellow or white onion, thinly sliced

1 recipe quantity Indian-Style Fusion Pinto Beans (see page 79)

Start by toasting the black chili in a frying pan over a medium heat for 5 seconds, or until it turns dark. Chop off the top and try to get rid of as many seeds as possible by tapping.

Bring 1.75 litres/60fl oz/7½ cups of water to the boil in a large saucepan and add the tomatoes, green chilies and garlic. Cook for about 8 minutes until the tomatoes soften. Add the stock cubes, black chilies and salt to taste and cook for another 3 minutes. Allow the mixture to cool and remove the peel from as many tomatoes as you can, before transferring to a blender and blitzing to a smooth paste. It should be a soupy consistency.

To season the sauce, heat the olive oil in a deep saucepan and add the tomato sauce. Cook for 4–5 minutes over a medium heat, then set aside.

To deep-fry the tortilla strips, heat the oil for frying in a saucepan over a medium heat. Working in batches so that you don't overcrowd the pan, add the tortilla strips to the oil. Turn the heat to medium-low and fry until crisp and golden. Remove from the pan using a slotted spoon and transfer to a plate lined with paper towels to drain.

To assemble, reheat the sauce in a saucepan for 3–4 minutes. Add the tortilla strips and stir in gently so they do not break.

Divide the mixture between 4 shallow bowls and garnish with the sour cream, sliced onions and pinto beans. Serve immediately. Any leftover mixture will keep in an airtight container for up to a week.

Spicy Pasta and Sweet Dal
Dal Dhokli

Dal dhokli is a well-loved Gujarati one-pot dish made with leftover dal and spiced dough. I know, it's shocking to think that there would be leftover dal, but it happens from time to time. It might seem a little time-consuming but trust me, it's worth it. The result is a harmonious blend of bold flavors from the spiced dumplings and the dal that'll leave you forgetting all about ravioli cooked in tomato sauce. Not only does it tantalize the taste buds, but it is jam-packed with nutritious goodness – the epitome of beauty inside and out.

SERVES 4

FOR THE SPICY DHOKLI (PASTA)

200g/7oz/1½ cups whole-wheat/wholemeal flour

2 tbsp besan (gram/chickpea flour)

3 tbsp oil, plus 2 tsp for greasing the dough

1 tsp ground turmeric

1½ tsp chili powder

½ tsp carom seeds (optional)

1½ tsp ground coriander-cumin powder (see page 20)

½ tsp salt

7–8 tbsp warm water

FOR THE SWEET DAL

Cooked dal (see page 119 for Gujarati Wedding Dal)

Salt, to taste

A small bunch of cilantro/coriander, chopped (optional)

TO SERVE

2–3 tbsp chopped red onion

A large handful of cilantro/coriander, chopped (optional)

3 tbsp fresh or frozen chopped green garlic or 1 tsp garlic paste

4 tsp groundnut (peanut) oil, for drizzling

Rice or roti, to serve

To make the spicy pasta, combine the flours and oil in a mixing bowl. Add the spices, salt and the warm water and mix until a shaggy dough forms. Knead the dough for 3–4 minutes until it is smooth, then add 2 teaspoons of oil and continue kneading for 2 more minutes.

Put the dal in a deep saucepan, add 720ml/24fl oz/3 cups of water, season with salt, and mix well. Bring the mixture to the boil over a medium heat, then reduce the heat to low. Let it simmer while continuing to make the pasta.

Divide the dough into 4 equal portions and shape each into round balls. Next, press each ball of dough flat between your palms, before rolling them into 20 x 25cm/8 x 10in discs on a flat surface.

Slowly drop the diamond-shaped dough into the dal a few at a time and let them simmer for 9–10 minutes. Once the pasta is cooked, stir in the chopped cilantro.

Spoon the dal into bowls and top with the onion, cilantro (if using) and green garlic or garlic paste (if using). Drizzle a little groundnut oil on top, then serve with rice or roti.

Kasuri Methi and Papad Curry

On a recent visit to India, I stumbled upon papad curry, and my taste buds (you know these taste buds of mine by now), wouldn't let me resist giving it a try. The flavor-rich desert region of Rajasthan is home to many scrumptious curries which aren't based on a plethora of veggies. I love that some curries are designed just to be packed with flavor and not centered around nutrition – sometimes I just want to think about my taste buds! To my joy, I discovered that it's quick and effortless to whip this curry up, taking only 10 minutes from start to finish. You can imagine how convenient this can be if you're short on time!

SERVES 4

3–4 tbsp vegetable, corn or groundnut (peanut) oil

1 tsp cumin seeds

Pinch of asafoetida (hing)

2–3 whole dried chilies

½ tsp ground turmeric

1½ tsp red chili powder

1½ tsp coriander-cumin powder (see page 20)

¾ tsp garam masala

3–4 tomatoes, grated

½ tsp salt

6 tbsp dried fenugreek leaves (kasuri methi)

6 papadam, broken into 5–7cm/2–3in pieces

Large handful of cilantro/ coriander leaves, chopped

2 tbsp fresh or frozen chopped green garlic (optional)

Chapati, to serve

Heat the oil in a saucepan and add the cumin seeds. When the seeds crackle, add the asafoetida and whole dried chilies. Turn the heat down and add the turmeric, chili powder and coriander-cumin powder to the pan and mix well. Add 360ml/12fl oz/1½ cups of water and bring to the boil. Stir in the garam masala and the tomatoes and season with salt. Stir continuously over a medium heat for 4–5 minutes, until everything is well combined. Add the fenugreek leaves and cook until the mixture is thickened to a curry consistency.

Just before serving, add the papadam pieces and stir in gently. Simmer for 2–3 minutes, then serve sprinkled with cilantro leaves and green garlic, if using, and serve with chapati.

Fenugreek with Garlic
Lasooni Methi

Lasooni methi is, without a doubt, one of the greatest dishes that we came across on our trip to Aurangabad, India. Originating in Maharashtra in the western peninsular region of India, this recipe follows the simple steps of simmering a healthy leafy green vegetable and acts as a flavour booster when added to vegetables.

SERVING 4

3 tbsp vegetable, corn or groundnut (peanut) oil

1½ tbsp chopped garlic

1 red onion, finely chopped

2 small green chilies, chopped

2 bunches of fenugreek leaves (methi), washed, dried, thick stems removed and chopped

2 tomatoes, deseeded and finely chopped

Large handful of cilantro/coriander leaves, finely chopped

Salt, to taste

Chapati or paratha, to serve

Heat the oil in a saucepan or wok over a medium-low heat, then add the garlic and sauté for 10–15 seconds until it turns light brown. Next, add the red onion and fry for 10 minutes until well softened. Add the green chilies and the methi leaves. Partially cover the pan with a lid and cook for 8–10 minutes until the leaves have softened.

Add the chopped tomatoes and the cilantro and season with salt. Mix everything together well. Cook this mixture for a further 2 minutes until the tomatoes have softened.

Serve with chapati or paratha.

Mushroom and Onion Tacos

This vegetarian taco recipe is a great addition to any meatless Monday recipe collection. Its simplicity is awe-inspiring, and the classic flavor is unforgettable. It has become a family dinner tradition.

SERVES 4

4½ tbsp oil, divided

1 yellow onion, thinly sliced

Salt, to taste

½ tsp oregano

½ tsp garlic powder

½ tsp ground black pepper

200g/7oz mushrooms, sliced

8 corn tortillas

320g/11¼oz mozzarella cheese, shredded (you can adjust this according to how much cheese you like in your tacos)

4–6 tbsp finely shredded Parmesan cheese

FOR THE SALSA

1 tbsp olive oil

2 tomatoes

4 tomatillos (green tomatoes)

2 small jalapeno peppers, stems removed

3 garlic cloves, peeled but left whole

1 small bunch of cilantro/coriander, chopped

¼ tsp ground black pepper

2 tsp lime juice

½ tsp salt

To make salsa, heat the oil in a heavy frying pan over a medium-low heat and fry the tomatoes, tomatillos, jalapeno peppers and garlic for 6–7 minutes until blackened. Once cooled, transfer them to a mortar and pestle and grind to a coarse consistency. Add the chopped cilantro and continue grinding for 2–3 minutes. Season with ground black pepper, lime juice and salt. Mix everything well. Transfer the salsa to a small bowl to serve alongside the tacos.

To cook the vegetables, heat 1 tbsp of the oil in a large frying pan and cook the onion for 2–3 minutes until soft. Season with salt and add ¼ tsp oregano, ¼ tsp garlic powder and ¼ tsp of the ground black pepper. Stir the spices into the onions, then transfer the onions to a plate and set aside. In the same pan, add another 1 tbsp of the oil and add the mushrooms, oregano, garlic powder and ground black pepper. Cook for 5–6 minutes until the mushroom slices are tender, then set aside.

To toast the tortillas, heat a large flat frying pan over a medium heat and add 2 teaspoons of oil. Once hot, add 2 tortillas to the pan and cook for 1½ minutes on each side until lightly golden. Add 3 tablespoons of mozzarella to each taco and let it melt before adding 4–5 slices of mushroom and onion on top. Gently press down on them using a spatula and cook for 10–15 seconds. Sprinkle Parmesan on top and cook for another 6–8 seconds, then remove from the pan. Repeat to cook the remaining tacos, then serve warm with the salsa.

Butter Paneer Malai

Malai paneer is a beloved Indian dish known for its soft and creamy texture. I struggled to recreate the dish in my bay area kitchen despite trying for years. I finally achieved the perfect recipe through trial and error, and using the right ingredients but adjusted for an American kitchen. The result is a dish that any family can enjoy in less than 30 minutes.

SERVES 4

2 tbsp unsalted butter

200g/7oz paneer, cut into 2.5cm/1in cubes

4 tbsp vegetable, corn or groundnut (peanut) oil

1 red onion, chopped

2 small Roma or vine tomatoes, chopped

12 cashew nuts

1 tsp chili powder

½ tsp ground turmeric

¾ tsp garam masala

¾ tsp ground coriander

1 tsp dried fenugreek leaves (kasuri methi)

3 tbsp heavy/double cream

Salt

Bread or rice, to serve

Melt the butter in a frying pan over a medium heat. Add the paneer and pan-fry for 5–6 minutes, turning the pieces now and then, until golden on all sides. Transfer the paneer to a bowl.

In the same wok, heat 3 tablespoons of the oil and fry the onion over a medium-low heat for 10–12 minutes until soft and lightly golden. Add the tomatoes and cashews, and fry for 5 minutes more. Remove the wok from the heat and leave the mixture to cool for 8–10 minutes. Transfer it to a blender and blitz to a purée.

Wipe the wok out with paper towels and set it over a medium heat. When hot, add the remaining 1 tablespoon of oil, the chili powder and turmeric and fry, stirring for 5 seconds. Add the purée, stir to combine with the oil and fry for 2 minutes. Add the garam masala, ground coriander and kasuri methi, and season with salt. Stir well until everything is combined. Add the paneer and 2 tablespoons of the cream, and cook for 4–5 minutes. Then stir in the remaining 1 tablespoon of cream, mixing well. Serve with your favorite bread or rice.

Tomato and Ghee Upma

Upma, a thick semolina porridge, is the perfect meal for a lazy day and reminds me of a cozy time from long ago. It's mouth-watering, healthy, and vibrant red will brighten even the cloudiest skies. This is the answer on those days when you need a bowl of true comfort food and a hit of vegetables. As a mother, I always want to ensure my family gets enough vegetables, so I make this dish often, as some of my family members are happy to guzzle it down in one go.

SERVES 4

140g/5oz/¾ cup coarse semolina (sooji)

2 tsp oil

35g/1¼oz/¼ cup raw peanuts

8–10 cashew nuts

3 tbsp ghee

1 tsp mustard seeds

1 tsp cumin seeds

Pinch of asafoetida (hing)

4–5 whole dried chilies

10–12 curry leaves

½ small red onion, chopped

1–2 green chilies, thinly sliced

1 tsp finely chopped fresh root ginger

1 carrot, finely chopped

50g/1¾oz/¼ cup green beans, chopped

4 tbsp fresh or frozen chopped green garlic

1½ tsp salt

3 tbsp tomato paste/puree

Large handful of cilantro/coriander, chopped

Tomato and Chana Dal Chutney (see page 158), to serve

Toast the semolina in a medium-sized deep pan over a medium heat for 4–5 minutes, stirring constantly, then transfer the toasted semolina to a bowl.

Heat 2 teaspoons of oil in the same pan, add the peanuts and cashews and cook for 1–2 minutes until they begin to turn a light golden colour. Transfer the nuts to a separate small bowl and set aside.

Heat 2 tablespoons of the ghee in the same pan and add the mustard seeds. Once the seeds crackle, add the cumin seeds, asafoetida, dried chilies and curry leaves and mix well. Add the onion and stir. Turn the heat to low and cook the onions for 5–6 minutes. Then turn the heat up to medium and add the green chilies and ginger and cook for 1–2 minutes, stirring continuously. Add the carrots and beans and cook for 4 minutes, or until the vegetables are tender.

Add 750ml/26fl oz/3 cups of water to the pan and bring the liquid to a boil. Add the green garlic and boil the mixture for 6 minutes. Pour in the toasted semolina and salt, mix, and cook for 2–3 minutes until well incorporated. Then add the tomato purée and mix well. Cover the pan and let it simmer for 3 minutes.

Top with the nuts, cilantro and the remaining ghee, and serve warm with tomato and chana dal chutney.

Gujarati Wedding Dal
Gujarati Lagan ni Dal

Wedding dal is a dish that holds a special place at Gujarati weddings. Also known as *lagan ni dal* or *vara ni dal*, it is cooked for longer, which gives it a rich depth of flavor. Back in the day, it was even served in a leaf bowl! This recipe takes me back to Gujarat, to a joyful wedding, surrounded by family and friends. Frozen yam is available at Indian supermarkets.

SERVES 4

180g/6½oz/1 cup yellow split pigeon peas (toor dal)

85g/3oz/½ cup yam (suran), diced into 5mm/¼in cubes (thaw if using frozen yam)

3 small tomatoes, chopped

6 tbsp shredded jaggery (gur) or brown sugar

3 tbsp fresh tamarind pulp (see page 48)

1½ tsp ground turmeric

4 tsp coriander-cumin powder (see page 20)

1 tbsp ginger paste

2 small green chilies, sliced

2¼ tsp salt

60g/2¼oz/⅓ cup peanuts

Handful of cilantro/coriander leaves, chopped

Rice or rotis, to serve

FOR THE SEASONING

4 tbsp groundnut (peanut) or corn oil

1½ tsp mustard seeds

½ tsp fenugreek seeds

3 whole red chilies, dried

½ tsp asafoetida (hing)

4 cloves

1 small stick of cinnamon

2 bay leaves

2 tsp red chili powder

Wash the split peas three times, then put them in a pressure cooker with the yam cubes and 1.5 litres/52fl oz/6½ cups of water. Cook under full pressure for 20–25 minutes. After allowing the pressure cooker to decompress, safely remove the lid and let the mixture cool slightly before whisking it well to a mushy and smooth consistency.

Transfer the mixture to a deep saucepan and add the tomatoes, jaggery, tamarind pulp, turmeric, coriander-cumin, ginger paste, green chilies, salt and 500ml/16fl oz/2 cups of water. Mix well, bring to the boil, then reduce the heat to medium-low and simmer for 7–8 minutes, stirring regularly. Add the peanuts and cook for 2–3 minutes.

To make the seasoning, heat the oil in a small saucepan over a medium heat. Add the mustard seeds and once they begin to crackle, add the fenugreek seeds, whole red chilies, asafoetida, cloves, cinnamon stick and bay leaves. Mix well and cook for 3–5 seconds. Turn the heat off and then add the chili powder. Immediately pour the seasoning over the dal. Add the cilantro and cook for 4–5 minutes, then serve with rice or rotis.

Note: You can also make this on the stovetop. Rinse the split peas three times, then put them in a pan with 2 litres/70fl oz/8½ cups of hot water and leave to soak for 4 hours. Bring the pan to a boil, skimming off any foam. Add the yam and cover and cook over a medium heat for about 1½ hours, or until the peas are very mushy.

Sri Lankan Dal

During our trip to Sri Lanka, my husband and I were excited to explore the country and its food. When we had an authentic Sri Lankan breakfast for the first time, it blew my mind; I loved everything they served, but the Sri Lankan dal was my favourite. I learned how to make it on the spot.

SERVES 4

260g/9oz/1½ cups split red lentils (lal masoor dal)

½ tsp ground turmeric

Salt, to taste

250ml/9fl oz/1 cup coconut milk

2 tbsp chopped cilantro/ coriander

1–2 tbsp rampe leaf (pandanus leaf), chopped

Rice, to serve

FOR THE SEASONING:

3 tbsp coconut oil

1 tsp mustard seeds

1 tsp cumin seeds

8–10 curry leaves

1 small cinnamon stick

2 whole dried red chilies

1 small red onion, sliced

4–5 garlic cloves, minced

2 tsp red chili powder or Kashmiri chili powder

Salt, to taste

Rinse the dal three times. Heat 1.5 litres/52fl oz/6½ cups of water in a deep saucepan over a high heat, add the rinsed dal and turmeric, and season with salt. Bring to the boil, then turn the heat down to medium and cook the dal for 25–30 minutes, or until the dal is very soft. Remove the pan from the heat and mash the dal with the back of a spoon until you have a creamy consistency. Add the coconut milk and mix well, then set aside.

For seasoning the dal, heat a frying pan over a medium heat and add the mustard seeds. When they crackle, add the cumin seeds, then the curry leaves, cinnamon stick, whole red chilies, onion and garlic. Cook for 7–8 minutes until the onion has softened, then add the chili powder, mix well, and cook for a further minute.

Add the seasoning to the dal mixture and bring to boil. Turn the heat down to low and simmer for 6–8 minutes until a creamy consistency is achieved. Stir in the cilantro and rampe leaves, if using. If the dal is too thick, add a splash of water.

Serve hot with rice.

Bean and Cheese Enchiladas

I came across this "most wanted" enchilada sauce recipe on my second trip to Puerto Vallarta, Mexico, thanks to the talented house chef. My family and I enjoyed it so much that we asked the chef to teach us how to make it. He was happy to share his recipe and even helped us purchase the necessary ingredients. I always recommend learning from local chefs or signing up for cooking classes to learn authentic dishes. They have the insider knowledge and expertise to create the most delicious meals. I've served this dish at many small dinner parties and received numerous compliments. My guests often ask for the recipe, so this is for you.

I've given two options for this recipe. One is the original, and one is a version I modified to suit my family's tastes. I encourage you to try Vina's twist, since using refried beans for the filling and flour tortillas instead of corn is a real crowd-pleasing adjustment. I have included both recipes below while keeping the enchilada sauce recipe the same.

SERVES 4

FOR THE ENCHILADA SAUCE
1 × 400G/14oz can of chopped tomatoes (or 4 large Roma tomatoes, boiled for 12 minutes, left to cool and skinned)
700ml/23½fl oz/3 cups chicken or vegetarian broth
4 tbsp olive oil
3 tbsp plain/all-purpose flour
1½ tsp chili powder
1 tsp dried oregano
1 tsp ground cumin
1 tsp sugar
½ tsp paprika (optional)
1 tsp salt

FOR THE ORIGINAL CORN ENCHILADAS
8 corn tortillas
227g/8oz/2 cups Tillamook sharp Cheddar cheese, preferably, or any Cheddar cheese, shredded, plus 8 tbsp to sprinkle on top of the enchiladas
4 tbsp black olives, chopped
4 tbsp mushrooms, chopped
1 bunch of scallions/spring onions, chopped, divided
1 tbsp sliced green chili (optional)
1 tbsp oil, plus extra for cooking the tortillas
Home-Style Refried Beans (see page 79), to serve

FOR THE ENCHILADAS WITH BEANS AND FLOUR TORTILLAS
8 medium-sized flour tortillas
260g/9oz/1 cup Home-Style Refried Beans (see page 79)
225g/8oz/1 cup Tillamook sharp Cheddar cheese, preferably, or any Cheddar cheese, shredded, plus 8 tbsp to sprinkle on top of the enchiladas
1 tbsp oil, plus extra for cooking the tortillas
4 tbsp chopped scallions/ spring onions, to sprinkle on top

RECIPE CONTINUES OVERLEAF

To make the enchilada sauce, if using canned tomatoes, combine the tomatoes and broth in a blender and blitz until smooth. If using fresh Roma tomatoes, combine the tomatoes and 700ml/24fl oz/3 cups of water in a saucepan and bring to the boil. Once at a boil, simmer for 4–5 minutes over a medium heat until the tomatoes have softened. Turn off the heat. Once cooled, take the tomatoes out of the water and remove their skins. Combine the tomatoes and broth in a blender and blitz until smooth.

Heat the oil in a medium-sized saucepan and add the flour. Cook for 1 minute, or until the flour turns light brown, while stirring constantly. Add the blended tomato mixture, chili powder, oregano, cumin, sugar and paprika (if using), and season with salt, to taste. Mix until well combined. Cook for 4–6 minutes until the sauce has a pouring consistency, adding a splash of water if it's too thick.

Next, roast your corn or flour tortillas. Heat a frying pan over a medium heat and grease it with 2 teaspoons of oil. One at a time, pan-fry each tortilla for 1½–2 minutes on each side until very light brown. Repeat the process with the remaining tortillas. Cover the tortillas with foil and set aside.

Preheat your oven to 190ºC/375ºF/Gas 5.

To make the Original Corn Enchiladas

To make the filling for the corn enchiladas, combine the cheese, olives, mushrooms, scallions/spring onions (reserving about 4 tablespoons of the green tops) and green chili, if using, in a bowl and mix well.

Grease a baking dish with the 1 tablespoon oil and then use 1 cup of the enchilada sauce to coat the baking dish.

Fill each corn tortilla with 2 tablespoons of the filling, then roll them up tightly, and arrange them side-by-side in the baking dish. Pour the rest of the enchilada sauce over the tortillas and sprinkle over the remaining green tops of the spring onions/scallions and the cheese. Bake in the oven for 8–10 minutes until the cheese is melted and bubbling. Serve warm with refried beans.

To make Flour Tortillas and Bean enchiladas

To make flour tortilla and bean enchiladas, grease the baking dish with the 1 tablespoon oil, then coat the pan with 1 cup of the enchilada sauce.

Fill each flour tortilla with 2 tablespoons of the refried bean and 2–3 tbsp of the cheese, then roll them up tightly, and arrange them side-by-side in the baking dish. Pour the remaining enchilada sauce over the tortillas and sprinkle the spring onions/scallions and the leftover grated cheese (approximately 12 tbsp) on top. Bake in the oven for 10–12 minutes until the cheese is melted and bubbling.

Serve warm.

Lemon Butter Sauce with Pasta

The recipe for buttery and lemony sauce has stood the test of time. My son Aamir, who grew up on pasta and Caesar salad, is an excellent cook himself, and he recently asked me to make this sauce. He had been craving it for over two decades and was surprised and delighted to learn that it is a simple sauce that requires minimal kitchen expertise. I like to add capers to the sauce to give it a tangy flavor.

SERVES 2

250ml/8fl oz/1 cup white wine

120ml/4fl oz/½ cup heavy/
  double cream

2 tbsp fresh lemon juice

2 tbsp capers

1 tsp salt

Pinch of ground black pepper

250g/9oz/2½ cups your
  choice of cooked pasta

10–12 basil leaves, cut
  lengthways, to garnish

Heat the saucepan over a medium heat, pour in the wine and bring to the boil. Reduce the wine until a quarter of the initial amount remains.

Add the cream and simmer for 5 minutes.

Add the lemon juice and mix well. Add the butter and constantly stir until it is melted and incorporated. Add the capers to the sauce and season with salt and pepper.

Add the cooked pasta to the sauce, plate up, and garnish with basil.

Note: If you want to add some protein to the dish, stir-fry 160g/5½oz of chicken breast with 1 tablespoon of butter for about 5 minutes until thoroughly cooked all the way through. Add it to the sauce.

Green Ravioli in Green Curry

Do you need a gourmet dinner that is bursting with flavor? One of my favorite dishes is spinach tortellini or small ravioli with coconut milk, seamlessly combining Thai and Italian flavors. This is a fantastic way to use store-bought tortellini in a surprising new invention! I often serve it plain or with other pasta dishes and my guests love it.

SERVES 4

200g/7oz ready-made fresh spinach tortellini or small ravioli

2 × 400g/14oz cans of coconut milk

3 tbsp green curry paste (store-bought, good-quality)

40g/1½oz/¼ cup shelled green peas or edamame beans

1 tbsp tamarind pulp (see page 48)

2 tbsp + 2 tsp sugar

½ tsp salt

5–6 green peppers, thinly sliced

6–7 Thai basil leaves, to serve

Cook the tortellini for a little less time than stated on the package instructions until they are cooked al dente, then set them aside.

Add the creamy part of the coconut milk that solidifies at the top of both of the cans to a deep pan and cook over a medium heat until the oil releases – this takes about 6–7 minutes.

Add the green curry paste and cook for 2 minutes until fragrant.

Add the remaining coconut milk and 120ml/4fl oz/½ cup of water to the pan. Add the cooked tortellini, green peas or edamame, and cook for 3–4 minutes.

Stir in the tamarind pulp and the sugar and season with salt. If the curry is too thick, add an extra splash of water. Add the sliced green peppers, mix well and turn off the heat. Leave the peppers to soften in the residual heat for 4 minutes before serving.

Serve hot, garnished with Thai basil leaves.

Fish & Meat

Whole Chicken Satay

For my chicken satay, I marinate the chicken in aromatic spices and coconut oil to make it juicy and tender. I prefer to cook the chicken whole, to make this completely effortless. You might have to adjust the spices depending on the size of your chicken. This recipe assumes the chicken is about 1¾kg/4lb. I've found that this homemade version is even more flavorful than takeout. If you can, start to marinate the chicken the day before you want to cook it. This dish is best served with my Coconut Rice on page 66.

SERVES 4

1 whole chicken (approximately 1¾kg/4lb)

FOR THE MARINADE:

400g/13½ oz/½ cup coconut cream

3 tbsp coconut oil, melted

3 tbsp curry powder

3 tbsp garlic paste

3 tbsp sugar

4 tbsp tamarind pulp (see page 48)

1½ tbsp red Thai curry paste

1 tsp ground black pepper

1 tbsp salt, or to taste

FOR THE PEANUT SAUCE:

1 tbsp peanut oil

100g/3½oz whole peanuts

2 pieces of candlenut, or 4 almonds, or 4 macadamia

2 garlic cloves, peeled

1 kaffir lime leaf

4 tsp soy sauce

180ml/6fl oz/¾ cup canned coconut milk

1 tbsp red or Panang curry paste

1 tbsp fish sauce (or ½ tsp salt)

4 – 5 tbsp palm sugar or brown sugar

1 tbsp tamarind pulp

Clean the chicken according to the manufacturer's instructions. Remove any giblets and rinse the chicken. Pat dry with a paper towel before marinating.

Place all the marinade ingredients in a mixing bowl and stir well to combine. Place the chicken along with the marinade in a baking pan, ensuring the chicken is well coated with the marinade. Poke the chicken with a fork to allow it to go deep into the flesh. Cover and leave in the refrigerator for 4–5 hours, or overnight for the best result.

Remove the chicken from the refrigerator 1 hour before cooking.

Preheat the oven to 200°C/400°F/Gas 6.

Place the chicken in the oven and turn the oven temperature down to 150°C/300°F/Gas 2. Bake for 1½-2 hours until it is tender and no longer pink.

In the meantime, make your peanut sauce. Heat the peanut oil in a small pan over a medium heat and add the peanuts. Fry the peanuts for 1-2 minutes, until they turn a light brown color. Add candlenuts or almonds or macadamia nuts and fry for 15-20 seconds, then add the garlic cloves and kaffir lime leaf and fry for 15-20 seconds.

Transfer the mixture to a mortar, add the soy sauce and 2 tablespoons of water, and grind until a smooth coarse paste forms. To finish the sauce, combine the paste with the rest of the peanut sauce ingredients and mix well.

Serve the chicken and sauce warm with coconut rice.

Andra-style Curry Leaf Chicken

This simple chicken curry is a cut above other homemade versions and has become a beloved family favorite, particularly with my daughter. My daughter's friend's mom, who is originally from Andrapradesh, visited me one afternoon and poured her love into showing me how to make this prized recipe. What a joy it is to cook with friends and to share in each other's knowledge.

The fresh curry leaves make all the difference, and if you prefer a dish without meat, replace the chicken with potatoes.

SERVES 4

570g/1lb 4oz skinless chicken
  breasts, cut into 5cm/2in
  chunks
1 large onion, roughly chopped
1 tsp ground turmeric
1 green chili, sliced in half
  lengthways
1½ tbsp garlic paste
1 tbsp ginger paste
3 tbsp oil
2 tsp mustard seeds
10 fresh curry leaves
2 dried red chilies
2½ tsp chili powder
¾ tsp salt
basmati or jasmine rice,
  to serve
3–4 tbsp chopped cilantro/
  coriander, to serve

FOR THE SPICE BLEND:
2 cloves
2 green cardamom pods
2 tbsp coriander seeds
Pinch of cumin seeds
¼ tsp ground cinnamon

For the spice blend, blitz all the ingredients to a fine powder in a spice grinder and set aside.

For the curry, bring approximately 750ml/26fl oz/3 cups of water to the boil in a large saucepan. Add the chicken chunks to the pan with the onion, turmeric, green chili, garlic and ginger pastes. Cover the pan and cook over a medium heat for 10–12 minutes, until the chicken is no longer pink.

Toward the end of the chicken simmering time, make a seasoning. Heat the oil in a frying pan and add the mustard seeds. Once they begin to crackle, add the curry leaves, red chilies, chili powder and the reserved spice blend. Mix well.

Add the seasoning to the pan of simmered chicken and mix well to combine. Cook over a low heat for 3–4 minutes until the sauce has thickened.

Season the dish with salt and serve with rice, sprinkled with cilantro.

Chicken Nachos

When I first made these chicken nachos for my kids' friends, I was pleasantly surprised to learn – from a mother who had been driving them – that they were raving about them. It was then that I realized my dish had become a popular topic of conversation among the kids at school. So this recipe is a tribute to my kids' wonderful friends, who appreciate and admire my cooking, Thank you, middle schoolers!

SERVES 4

3 tbsp oil

320g/11½oz ground/minced chicken breast

3 tbsp taco seasoning

120g/4¼oz corn chips

180g/6¼oz/2 cups shredded Cheddar cheese

115g/4oz/½ cup pickled jalapeños, sliced (add more if you like spicy)

Small bunch of scallions/spring onions, thinly sliced

Preheat the oven to 180ºC/350˚F/Gas 4.

Heat the oil in a large frying pan over a medium-high heat. Add the chicken and cook for 4 minutes until it is no longer pink. Add the taco seasoning and mix well. Cook for 2 more minutes, stirring continuously.

To assemble the nachos, arrange the corn chips on a flat baking sheet. Scatter the chicken, Cheddar and pickled jalapeños on top of the corn chips to cover them. Bake for 5–7 minutes, or until the cheese starts melting.

Remove from the oven, sprinkle the sliced scallions on top and serve warm.

THE HERBS AND SPICES OF THAILAND

My daughter Elissa and I took a trip to Thailand in February 2012. What a treat! Our family-favorite dishes include Thai classics such as Tom Kha Tofu, Panang Curry and Sticky Mango Rice. The trip had a profound impact on me.

My first encounter with Thai food was in 1989, when I came to America and my husband took me to a local Thai restaurant in India. But the smell and taste were so new to me that I almost left. However, my husband encouraged me to try a little of everything, and over the years I learned to love this fragrant cuisine.

I decided to take Thai cooking lessons in 1995, and it turned out to be one of the best decisions I ever made. During those few weeks, I learned a lot about Thai ingredients and techniques. Since then I've invited friends over and taught them Thai curry and other dishes. One touching incident involved a friend who came to my cooking lesson and gave the leftover curry to her friend's fifteen-year-old son who was battling cancer. He adored the curry, and I received a call from the same friend informing me how much he enjoyed the home-cooked Thai food. It brought me great happiness.

My daughter's friend, Monish, is a huge fan of my Basil and Garlic Chicken, which is inspired by Thai flavors. I made this dish for Monish the first time he visited our home and he fell in love with it so deeply that he asked me if I would teach him the recipe. A month after our special cookery lesson, Monish sent me a text. He had met a lovely girl and decided to make her the dish for their date. She was so impressed that she agreed to a second date. Monish sent me a photo of the beautiful girl along with a message: "I made the Thai chicken for the girl I'm dating, and she loved it so much. Now, in your book, you can say your recipes can find you a girlfriend."

I sat there smiling and wondered perhaps if Tinder had my recipes they'd be even more successful in matchmaking. Monish said he prepared it again for their two-month dating anniversary. While I can't guarantee romance will blossom from these recipes, I can tell you that food has the power to bring people together!

Key herbs and spices in Thai cooking:

🌾 **TAMARIND** – see Thai-inspired Whole Roast Chicken on page 130

🌾 **THAI BASIL** – see Steamed Fish with Basil Sauce on page 146, Green Ravioli in Green Curry on page 127

🌾 **CHILI** – see Papaya Salad on page 84, Basil and Garlic Chicken on page 136

🌾 **COCONUT** – see Coconut Rice with Pomegranate on page 66, Chocolate Chip Coconut Bars on page 162

Basil and Garlic Chicken

This is the very special second-date-securing chicken dish. I believe that food has the power to bring people together, so try cooking this one for a loved one and see how it goes … Love is Served!

My girls also love this recipe with ground pork instead of chicken, so I highly recommend you try it with pork as well.

SERVES 4

4 tbsp peanut oil

3 tbsp finely chopped garlic

570g/1¼lb ground/minced chicken thighs or pork

2 tbsp grated green chili

3 tbsp soy sauce

2 tbsp brown sugar

10–12 basil leaves, roughly chopped, plus extra to garnish

4–5 jalapeño chili slices, to garnish (optional)

Rice, to serve

Heat the oil in a frying pan over a medium heat. Add the garlic and cook until caramelized, then add the meat and stir-fry for 3–4 minutes, stirring continuously.

Add the green chili and stir to combine. Push the mixture to the side of the pan and add the soy sauce and brown sugar. Cook until bubbling, then mix into the meat mixture. Reduce the heat to low and stir in the basil leaves, cooking until the basil begins to wilt.

Garnish with basil leaves and jalapeño slices, if using.

Serve warm with rice.

Fiery Fish Forever

This is an original Vina Patel, created one day when I was craving a simple fish dish and had several of my favorite ingredients to hand. It's handy for my kids too, as I can prepare the marinade and send it off to college with them, safe in the knowledge that they need to buy only the fresh salmon to finish it, but mostly because they have a healthy meal that reminds them of home.

SERVES 4

4 skin-on salmon fillets (approximately 600g/1⅓lb in total)

1½ tbsp garlic paste

1½ tbsp cayenne pepper or chili powder

1½ tbsp cumin-coriander powder (see page 20)

1 tsp salt

juice of 2 lemons

3 tbsp butter, for frying

Run the salmon fillets under cold water, then pat them dry with kitchen paper.

In a small bowl, combine the garlic paste, cayenne pepper, cumin-coriander powder and salt. Add the lemon juice and mix well, then pour the marinade over the salmon fillets. Poke the salmon with a fork so that the marinade goes deep into the flesh, then turn the fillets skin-side up. Cover and place in the refrigerator for 2–4 hours, or overnight.

Heat a frying pan for 3 mintues over a medium heat, then add 1½ tablespoons of the butter. Once the butter starts foaming, add 2 fish fillets, skin-side up. Cover the pan and cook for 5 minutes. Turn the fish over and cook for another 3–4 minutes, or until the skin is brown. Repeat the process with the remaining 2 fillets.

Serve the salmon warm.

Salmon with Chipotle Sauce

On our travels in Mexico, we have been fortunate to discover many culinary delights. This recipe was inspired by a dish we found in Puerto Vallarta, a place which left a lasting impression on us with its vibrant food culture and warm hospitality. This dish of smoky chipotle sauce and juicy salmon will transport you to the warm beaches of Mexico.

SERVES 4

600g/1½lb salmon, divided into 4 portions

½ tsp salt

Pinch of black pepper

½ x 220g/7½oz can of La Costena Chipotle chili, or 1½ tbsp chipotle chili paste

4 tbsp lime juice

4 tbsp honey

Small bunch of cilantro/ coriander, chopped

2 tbsp melted butter

Pasta or salad, to serve

Preheat the oven to 190ºC/375ºF/Gas 5.

Place the salmon fillets in a baking dish, and sprinkle with the salt and pepper.

To make the chipotle sauce, combine the chili, lime juice, honey, cilantro and butter in a bowl. Pour the chipotle sauce over the salmon fillets.

Bake the salmon for 15 minutes. Then serve with your choice of pasta or salad.

Shrimp/Prawn Penne with Basil, Garlic and Oyster Sauce

This is such a simple dish to entertain your guests, and the best part about it is the amount of vegetables and garlic used in the recipe – it's a great way to add more greens to your diet. You can use any pasta that suits your dietary requirements and it will still taste amazing.

SERVES 4

4 tbsp peanut oil

2 tbsp finely chopped garlic

2 tbsp finely chopped green chili

210g/7½oz raw shrimp/ prawns, tails removed and shelled

2 tbsp oyster sauce

200g/7oz broccoli, cut into small pieces

210g/7½oz penne pasta

Salt, to taste

8–10 mint leaves, roughly chopped

10–12 Thai basil leaves, roughly chopped

Heat the oil in a wok/frying pan over a medium heat. Once hot, add the garlic and cook for 10–15 seconds until caramelized. Add the chili and cook for 5 seconds. Add the shrimp and cook for 3–4 minutes. Add the oyster sauce, mix well and cook for 1–2 minutes. Add the broccoli and cook for 2–3 minutes. Turn the heat off.

Cook the pasta in a saucepan according to the package instructions, then drain.

Add the pasta to the pan with the shrimp and mix well. Cook for 2–3 minutes over a medium heat. Season with salt if it needs it.

Add the mint and basil leaves, and serve hot.

Keralan–Style Shrimp/Prawns

My heart swelled with pride when my son's friend tried this dish and said, "This is probably the best shrimp dish I've ever had."

After an intense and atmospheric photoshoot in Gujarat for my first cookbook, *From Gujarat with Love*, my husband and I took a trip to Kerala, "God's Country", in July 2019. Our highlights were a tour of the spice garden, where we learned a lot about Indian spices and how to grow them, and staying in beautiful tea garden villas with panoramic views. On the day we arrived, my husband ordered coconut shrimp curry and it was so delicious that when we got home, I experimented until I had perfected the recipe.

The key ingredient in this recipe is fresh coconut slices.

SERVES 4

2 tsp chili powder

½ tsp ground turmeric

1 tbsp ground coriander

2 tsp ginger paste

1 tbsp garlic paste

4 tbsp rice flour

½ tsp salt

400g/14oz raw shrimp/prawns, tails removed and shelled

6–8 tbsp oil

12–15 curry leaves

70g/2½oz fresh coconut, sliced

Coconut Rice with Pomegranate (see page 66)

Combine the chili powder, ground turmeric, ground coriander, ginger and garlic pastes, rice flour, salt and 1½ tablespoons of water in a medium bowl. Add the shrimp and mix until they are well coated.

Heat the oil in a shallow frying pan over a medium heat. Add the curry leaves and fry for 3–5 seconds until soft. Add the coconut slices and fry for 10–15 seconds. Remove the curry leaves and coconut slices from the oil using a skimmer and transfer them to a small bowl. Keep aside.

Add the shrimp to the pan and cook for 2 minutes on one side. Flip them and cook for another minute until they are cooked through and lightly golden.

Add the reserved curry leaves and coconut slices back into the pan and mix gently. Cook for a further minute.

If there is any excess oil, you can drain it off before serving. Serve warm with coconut rice.

Garlic Shrimp/Prawn Tacos

Are you looking to make weeknight supper in five minutes? My shrimp tacos are a total blockbuster and have received five glowing stars from my family. The combination of shrimp and taco sauce is like Bonnie and Clyde – a powerful duo. The secret to my divine sauce is garlic paste, which adds a touch of garlicky goodness and elevates every dish to new heights of deliciousness. Garlic shrimp/prawns offer so much flavor, you can sometimes enjoy eating them straight from the wok, without condiments or tortillas.

SERVES 4

4 tbsp butter

2 tbsp minced garlic

250g/8½oz raw shrimp/prawns,
   tails removed and shelled

1 tsp chili powder, to taste

1½ tbsp taco seasoning

3 tbsp finely chopped parsley

8 soft corn tortillas

2 tbsp oil

1 red onion, thinly sliced,
   to serve (optional)

FOR THE BAJA SAUCE:

125g/4½oz/½ cup mayonnaise

125g/4½oz/½ cup sour cream

2 tsp garlic paste

1 tbsp lime juice

1 tsp ground black pepper

2 tbsp finely chopped parsley

Salt, to taste

FOR THE TACO SEASONING:

2 tbsp chili powder

1 tbsp ground cumin

1 tsp paprika or ½ tsp
   ground cayenne pepper

1 tsp garlic powder

1 tsp onion powder

½ tsp dried oregano

Pinch of salt and pepper

Combine all the ingredients for the taco seasoning in a small bowl and mix well until combined. It can be stored in a small jar.

For the baja sauce, combine all the ingredients in a bowl and mix well. Add salt to taste, and set aside.

For the shrimp, heat a wok over a medium heat and add the butter and garlic. Fry until the garlic is pale gold, but be careful not to let it burn. Add the shrimp and cook for about 2–3 minutes until they start to turn pink. Add the chili powder and taco seasoning and cook for another 2 minutes until the shrimp are cooked through. Remove the pan from heat and stir in the parsley.

To toast the tortillas, heat 1 teaspoon of oil in a frying pan and cook a tortilla on each side for 1–2 minutes. Repeat the process to cook the remaining tortillas, covering the toasted tortillas with kitchen foil to keep them warm.

To assemble, spread 2 teaspoons of the baja sauce across a toasted tortilla and place 2–3 shrimp on top. Sprinkle with red onion slices, if using, and serve warm to appreciate its full flavors.

Steamed Fish with Basil Sauce

This deeply delicious (and added-fat-free!) steamed dish truly is a breath of fresh air. It uses an incredible combination of ingredients such as Thai basil and garlic, and the delicate texture of the fish is preserved as it gently steams, absorbing all the flavours – resulting in an outstanding dish that takes no longer than 10 minutes to make. The genius behind the dish is my darling husband, so he deserves full credit here. I have offered Swiss chard leaves as an alternative if you cannot source banana leaves, but it's helpful to know that banana leaves can be found in the frozen section of Asian supermarkets, so it's worth looking out for them.

SERVES 4

4 banana leaves (or 4 large Swiss chard or collard green leaves)

4 skinless and boneless tilapia fillets (approximately 500g/17½oz)

FOR THE BASIL SAUCE:

3 tbsp minced garlic

3 tbsp finely chopped green chili

3 tbsp oyster sauce

¼ tsp salt

10 Thai basil leaves, chopped

8 cilantro/coriander sprigs

Rice, to serve

Wash the banana leaves with cold water and pat dry with paper towels, then trim them into two 20cm/8in squares. Place a fish fillet onto each banana leaf – you will be making 4 separate parcels. Combine the garlic, green chili, oyster sauce and salt in a small bowl and spoon a quarter of the sauce over each piece of fish. Divide the basil leaves and cilantro sprigs between the parcels, then fold the top and bottom edges of each of the banana leaves over the fish, followed by the sides, enclosing the fish completely. If they are opening up, you can use a toothpick to secure them.

To steam the fish, add 1.5 litres/52fl oz/6½ cups of water to a steamer over a medium heat. If you don't have a steamer, place a steamer rack or basket in a pan of boiling water. Place the fish parcels into the steamer without overlapping them. Cover with a lid to trap the steam. Leave to steam for approximately 8–10 minutes, or until the fish is fully cooked through.

Serve the fish with rice.

Dips & Pickles

Sweet Mango Pickle
(Gur Keri)

My mother's sweet mango pickle recipe is exceptional, as she infuses it with love. Being a Gujarati, I have a particular fondness for sweet pickles. Try this quick and easy recipe for a spicy and tangy Indian pickle without the long marination process. Make mom's special pickle recipe once, and you'll never go back to store-bought again.

Sweet and sour pickle is more than a condiment; it is a way of life, as no meal is complete without a pickle. Pickle brings incredible energy to food and to every dish that you are eating. I have the most magical memories of pickles, as my mom would pack a jar with us whenever we took a trip. I love that pickle is a taste of home and that it can really double up your joy while traveling. It can be said that all you really need is a jar of good homemade pickles.

MAKES APPROX. 600G/1¼LB

2 large unripe mangos, peeled and diced

2 tsp salt, plus more to taste

480ml/16fl oz/2 cups peanut oil

Pinch of asafoetida (hing)

415g/14½oz pickle masala (readily available at Indian supermarkets)

175g/6¼ oz/¾ cup grated jaggery, or less if you like your pickle less sweet

Masala Poori, to serve (see page 36)

Put the diced mango and salt in a bowl and gently stir to combine. Set aside for an hour to allow the mangos to release their juices. Using your hands, gently squeeze the excess juice from the mango and discard the juice. Using paper towels, remove any remaining juice and spread the mango out on a large plate. Leave to dry in the sun or a warm, dry place for 3–5 hours. Transfer the diced mango to a bowl.

Heat the oil in a deep pan over a low heat for 10 minutes. Add the asafoetida, then remove the pan from the heat and set aside to cool completely. Once cool, add the pickle masala and jaggery and stir well. Add the diced mango and stir well again. Add salt if needed. Transfer the mango pickle to a jar.

Store the jar in a dark place for 2 days for the pickle to marinate. Stir before serving. Serve with masala poori. Keep the pickle in the refrigerator for up to 2 months.

Mango and Date Chutney

I am very grateful to my elder sister for introducing me to this recipe, as it offers a way to make chutney without adding sugar, but still manages to achieve that sweet and sour balance. If you are an ethnic cook from India, you will know how challenging this can be when making chutneys.

**MAKES APPROX.
280G / 10OZ / 1 CUP**

2 tbsp mango powder
(amchur powder)
9 dates, pitted
½ tsp cumin seeds
¼ tsp chili powder
¼ tsp salt

Combine the mango powder in small saucepan with 480ml/16oz/2 cups of water and bring it to the boil over a medium heat. Add the dates, cumin seeds, chili powder and salt and cook for 5–6 minutes. Let the mixture cool off before blending to a smooth paste.

Transfer the chutney to an airtight container. It can be stored in the refrigerator for up to a week.

Stuffed Mango Pickle
(Dabda)

In my family, we have some amazing cooks who are experts at making the most delicious pickles. This recipe has been passed down through the generations; secrets have been shared with me, making this recipe a true family collaboration. You'll be amazed by the stunning, vibrant color and unique sour and spicy flavor of these whole mangos pickled in masala. They make for a great alternative to regular pickles and are the perfect condiment.

MAKES APPROX. 800G/1¾LB

8–10 raw small or baby
  mangos
200g/7oz pickle masala
  (readily available at Indian
  supermarkets)
½ tsp salt
375ml/13fl oz/2 cups peanut
  oil

Wash and dry the mangoes, then remove the tops. Using a sharp knife, make two crosscuts on the top of one of the mangoes, then run the knife down the length. After opening the incision, carefully remove the seed, leaving the mango whole. Repeat this process with the remaining mangoes.

Combine the pickle masala and salt in a bowl. Stuff each mango with 2 tablespoons of the pickle masala and place the stuffed mangos in a deep bowl, cut-side up. Any leftover pickle masala should be sprinkled on top.

Heat the oil in a small pan over a low heat for 10 minutes. Remove the pan from the heat and set aside to cool completely.

Once the oil has cooled, pour it over the stuffed mangos, turning them over in the oil, then cover and place the dish in a dark place and leave to marinate for 2 days.

Transfer the pickle to an airtight jar and store it in the refrigerator for up to 2 months.

Note: This is an approximate weigh as actual weights may very slightly.

Garlic Pickle with Fenugreek and Black Gram
(Methi Chana and Garlic Achar)

Back home, our neighbor across the street introduced my family to this healthy and wholesome pickle. I fell in love with it at first bite, and it has stayed with me all my life. An Indian person's lunch and dinner can only be complete and truly fulfilling when served alongside mango pickles. I'm particularly a fan of this recipe, as it's packed with the health benefits from the fenugreek seeds and garlic, including inflammation-reducing and immune-boosting properties.

MAKES APPROX. 600G/2OZ

1 medium unripe
  mango, peeled and diced
  into 5mm/¼in cubes
1¼ tsp salt
55g/2oz/¼ cup black gram
  (kala chana)
50g/1¾ oz/¼ cup fenugreek
  seeds (methi seeds)
250ml/9fl oz/1 cup peanut oil
12–14 garlic cloves,
  thickly sliced
6 tbsp pickle masala
  (readily available at Indian
  supermarkets)

Combine the mango and salt in a bowl and set aside for 2 hours to allow the mango to release its water.

Meanwhile, using a colander, wash and drain the black gram and transfer to a small bowl. Also wash and drain the fenugreek seeds and transfer to a different small bowl. Combine the Bengal gram and the fenugreek seeds in with the mango. Allow everything to soak for 4–5 hours.

Drain the mix, then spread it out on a large plate and let it air dry for 3–4 hours.

Heat the oil in a small pan over a low heat for 4 minutes. Turn off the heat and then add the garlic and allow it to cook for 1 minute. Add the pickle masala and mix well, then add the mango mixture and stir until everything is well combined.

Transfer the pickle to an airtight glass jar and cover with the lid. Let it sit for 2 days at room temperature to infuse before serving. Store the pickle in a refrigerator for up to a month.

Note: This is an approximate weight as actual weights may very slightly.

Carrot Raita with Toasted Cumin Seeds

Raita is a very important condiment served in every part of India. A good raita – for example this carrot raita – can make an excellent side dishes for curry or dal.

SERVES 4

1 tbsp cumin seeds
425g/15oz/2 cups yogurt
½ tsp salt
1 small onion, finely chopped
1 carrot, peeled and grated
1 small beet/beetroot, cooked
   and grated, to garnish

To toast the cumin seeds, heat a small heavy-based pan over a low heat. Add the cumin seeds and dry roast them for 2–3 minutes until they start releasing an aroma, stirring continuously.

Remove the pan from the heat and let them cool, then grind most of the seeds in a mortar and pestle or grinder to make a coarse powder.

To make the raita, combine the yogurt with 125ml/4fl oz/ ½ cup of water and whisk until smooth. Add 1 tablespoon of the roasted cumin powder, season with salt and whisk again. Add the onion and carrots and stir them into the yogurt until well mixed.

Sprinkle the remaining roasted cumin powder and grated beet on top of the raita. Serve chilled as a side dish.

Tomato and Chana Dal Chutney

One of my all-time favorite dishes to make at home is this coconut-based tomato and chana dal chutney. It's a simple and speedy recipe that can be whipped up in the comfort of your own home. I love pairing it with plain rice because the creamy texture from Bengal gram is incredibly satisfying and filling, and it also goes well with my Mung Sprout Crepes (see page 38).

MAKES 250ML/9FL OZ/1 CUP

1 tbsp coconut oil

1 tsp cumin seeds

4 tbsp split Bengal gram (chana dal)

2–3 red chilies, depending how hot you want your chutney

10–12 curry leaves

4 Roma or vine tomatoes, roughly chopped

Salt, to taste

FOR THE SEASONING

2 tsp coconut oil

1 tsp mustard seeds

2 dried red chilies

6–8 curry leaves

Heat the oil in a saucepan over a medium heat. Add the cumin seeds and, once they crackle, add the Bengal gram and red chilies and sauté for 2–4 minutes. Add the curry leaves and tomatoes to the pan, mix well and cook for 8–10 minutes until the raw tomato flavour is gone.

Remove the chutney from the heat and let it cool. Transfer the mixture to a blender or food processor and grind it to a paste, then season with salt to taste and mix well. Transfer the chutney to a small bowl.

For the seasoning, heat the coconut oil in a small pan and, once hot, add the mustard seeds. Once the seeds start to crackle, add the dried red chilies and curry leaves. Cook for 3–5 seconds, then pour the seasoning over the tomato and chana dal chutney and serve.

Mint Chutney with Garlic

Condiments are a staple in many Indian households and are served with almost every meal. I love experimenting with different condiments, which add some extra flavour to my meals. One of my favorites is this mint chutney that I really enjoy with samosas.

MAKES 250ML/9FL OZ/1 CUP

2 bunches of mint leaves

1 bunch of cilantro/coriander

4 garlic cloves, peeled but left whole

3cm/1in piece of ginger, peeled

2 green chilies

2 tbsp lime juice

1 tsp salt

4 tbsp water

Combine all the ingredients in a blender or food processor and blend to a smooth paste.

Transfer the chutney to an airtight jar and store in the refrigerator for up to a week.

Sweet Things

Chocolate Chip Coconut Bars

In my house, we call these mouthwatering chocolate chip coconut bars "Patel Family Bars" since they have made a regular appearance for 30 years during Christmas. This treasured family recipe originally came from a dear friend who happily shared it with me after making them for us many times. It seems like those magic bars have a special power and disappear quickly. A delightful character nicknamed RigaToni is a new addition to your family and seems to have a special love for these cute squares. It's quite impressive that he ate them for breakfast, lunch, and dinner. Although he may feel a little guilty, he can't resist reaching for more from the jar. I look forward to making more and creating more smiles. They disappear so fast. Once you make them, watch your family fight for the last bar in the batch.

MAKES: 24-26 SQUARES

450g/1lb digestive biscuits (graham crackers)

266g/10oz/1¼ cup butter, melted, plus 2 tbsp for greasing

350g/12¼oz/1¾ cups semi-sweet/ milk chocolate chips

155g/5½oz/1½ cups sweetened coconut flakes

255g/9oz sweetened condensed milk

Preheat your oven to 160°C/325°F/Gas 3.

Blitz the biscuits in a food processor until they become fine crumbs. Set aside.

Grease a 30cm x 25cm/12in x 10in baking pan with 1 tbsp of the melted butter.

Combine the rest of the butter with the biscuit crumbs and mix well, then transfer to the baking pan. Spread the mixture out evenly, then press down with a potato masher to form a solid layer. Bake for 12 minutes, then remove and let it cool for an hour.

Sprinkle the chocolate chips evenly over the biscuit base, followed by the coconut flakes. Drizzle the condensed milk over the top to create an even layer. Bake for 25–30 minutes until the top turns light golden brown.

Remove from the oven and allow to cool completely. Cut into 5cm/2in squares and store in an airtight container.

Guilt-free and Gluten-free Vegan Chocolate Chip Cookies

Guilt-free and gluten-free chocolate cookies are a rare find, so I have some exciting news for those with a sweet tooth! I discovered these while at a retreat center in Costa Rica and was thrilled to learn that there was a cooking class available to learn how to make them. I eagerly signed up and have been enjoying pairing them with a warm cup of masala chai ever since. This delicious combination satisfies my craving for something sweet without causing a spike in blood sugar levels.

MAKES 12–14

Cooking spray or 4–5 tsp oil, to grease the baking tray

300g/10½oz/2 cups whole almonds

100g/3½oz/½ cup coconut sugar

5 tbsp coconut milk

1 tsp baking soda/bicarbonate of soda

Pinch of salt

120g/4¼oz/¾ cup chocolate chips

Preheat the oven to 180ºC/350ºF/Gas 4 and grease a baking sheet.

Blend the almonds in a food processor to make a powder.

Combine all the ingredients in a large mixing bowl and mix well to form a dough.

Using an ice cream scoop (or scoop 2 tablespoons of the mixture per cookie), form the dough into balls and place them on the prepared baking sheet.

Bake for 12 minutes until the tops are firm. Remove the cookies from the oven and serve warm.

Brown Rice Pancakes with Almond Milk

A few years back, I used to volunteer at my daughter's preschool once a week. My role involved spending time with the kids throughout the day and cooking for them. Occasionally, the mums could taste the food on offer, and these brown rice flour pancakes made with almond milk always went down well with them. I continued to make these pancakes for many years, even as my children got older and moved on. I add a pinch of ground turmeric to get a vibrant colour. And they're not just desserts – they make the perfect sweet snack.

MAKES 8-10 PANCAKES

85g/3oz/½ cup brown rice flour
Pinch of salt
1 tbsp brown sugar or honey
1 egg, beaten
180ml/6fl oz/¾ cup sweetened almond milk
Handful of blueberries
2 tbsp chocolate chips
Oil, to cook the pancakes
Fresh berries of your choice, to serve

In a mixing bowl, combine the brown rice flour, salt and sugar or honey. Add the beaten egg and the almond milk and whisk well until there are no lumps in the batter. Add the blueberries and chocolate chips, then stir gently.

Heat a non-stick pan over a medium heat and add a drizzle of oil. Drop 2 tablespoons of the batter into the hot pan and use a circular motion to spread the batter into a circular shape about 7.5cm/3in in diameter. Cook for 1–2 minutes, then carefully flip the pancake and cook on the other side for another minute until it turns light golden. Remove the pancake from the pan and serve warm. Repeat the process with the remaining batter until all the pancakes have been made.

Serve warm as they are or scattered with fresh berries.

Cardamom and Rose Perfumed Baklava

Roses and baklava never fail to delight me. Though I love all types of sweets, when it comes to baklava, there's only one type I'll eat: my cardamon and rose baklava. A dear Persian friend taught me how to make baklava, so this recipe holds sentimental value for me. The influence of Persian culture on Indian cuisine is evident in the use of cardamom and rosewater in my mother's cooking. Each bite of this nutty, sweet and rose-scented delicacy is infused with nostalgia.

MAKES 20–25 PIECES

400g/14oz/2 cups sugar

A few drops of rose extract or essence, available at Indian supermarkets

450g/1lb/2 cups unsalted butter, melted, plus extra for greasing

375g/13oz/3 cups pecans, coarsely ground

3 tbsp ground cardamom

14 sheets of filo/phyllo pastry

1½ tbsp edible rose petals, coarsely ground, to garnish

Preheat the oven to 180°C/350°F/ Gas 4.

To make the syrup, combine 480ml/16fl oz/2 cups of water and the sugar in a saucepan and bring to the boil over a medium-high heat. Stir until the sugar dissolves, then reduce the heat to medium and simmer for 12–15 minutes, or until reduced and you see a string form when you lift the spoon from the syrup. Remove the pan from the heat and stir in the rose water or extract. Set aside to cool.

Grease a 30cm x 40cm/12in x 16in baking pan with butter.

Combine the pecans and cardamom in a small bowl. Lay a sheet of pastry in the prepared baking tin, trimming it to make sure it fits properly inside. Brush it generously with melted butter, then repeat the process with another sheet of pastry, buttering it before adding another layer, until you've layered up 7 sheets. Spread the pecan mixture evenly over the top of the pastry, then continue layering and buttering until you've used up another 7 sheets.

Using a sharp knife, cut the baklava into a grid of diamond shapes, each 4cm/1½in wide. Place the tin in the middle of the oven and bake for 25–30 minutes until it turns golden brown.

Remove from the oven and pour the cooled syrup on top, then let it cool completely. Sprinkle the rose petals on top to serve. Store the baklava in an airtight container for up to 2 weeks.

Custard-Flavored Fruit Salad

My fruit salad is a wonderful make-ahead dessert that I've prepared for so many of my get-togethers. It's almost always the talk of the party, and I get repeat requests for it. My folks love this dish, as it's light and full of juicy and refreshing fresh fruit. The bananas offer plenty of rich natural sweetness, while the pomegranate seeds bring an exciting crunch and tang. This recipe is laden with wellness-giving goodness and is a perfect pudding to serve at your next gathering.

SERVES 6

12–15 almonds

2 litres/70fl oz/8½ cups whole milk

2 tbsp custard powder

5–7 tbsp sugar

1 tsp ground cardamom

1 red apple, cut into 1cm/ ½in dice

1 banana, cut into 1cm/ ½in dice

85g/3oz/½ cup pomegranate seeds

60–85g/2–3oz seedless grapes, halved

Boil 250ml/9fl oz/1 cup of water in a small pan. Remove the pan from the heat and add the almonds. Let them soak for 1 hour before draining, peeling and slicing them. Set aside.

Pour the milk into a deep saucepan over a high heat and bring to the boil. Reduce the heat to low, cover the pan with a lid and cook for 50 minutes–1 hour, stirring every 10 minutes. Remove the pan from the heat and let it cool.

After the milk has cooled down, you can use it to prepare custard milk.

To make custard milk, take only 3–4 tablespoons of the cooked milk and pour them into a small separate bowl. Add the custard powder to the milk in the bowl and whisk it well until there are no lumps. Add this mixture back into the remaining milk. Now add the sugar, cardamom, almond slices, and all the fruits, and mix well to combine all the ingredients. Transfer the fruit salad to a serving bowl and cover. Place the bowl in the refrigerator and chill for 2–4 hours.

Serve the fruit salad chilled.

Indian Mango Pie

This is the easiest dessert recipe you'll find in my collections, courtesy of another mom friend of mine, who has happily shared this recipe with pure love. I highly recommend using canned kesar mango pulp for a more vibrant and intense Indian mango flavor.

SERVES 10–12

170g/6oz jelly cubes/Jell-O gelatin, peach or orange flavor

225g/8oz canned condensed milk

880g/30oz canned mango pulp (kesar, if possible)

235ml/8oz double/heavy cream, whipped

2 pie crusts, premade and baked

Bring 350ml/12fl oz/1½ cups of water to the boil in a medium-sized deep saucepan. Remove the pan from the heat and let it cool. Once cooled, whisk in the remaining ingredients and divide the mixture equally between the two pie crusts. Refrigerate the pies for 2–4 hours. Serve chilled.

Leftover pie can be frozen for up to 3 months.

Ghughra Pie

Ghughra, also known as "Ghugiya", is a must-have Diwali sweet in Gujarat and a Holi sweet that is enjoyed all over India. Diwali without Ghughra is incomplete. In this recipe, I have given traditional ghughra a modern look, while using authentic ingredients, to trim down the number of steps and cut down on the amount of fats usually used.

Diwali is an auspicious festival in India. On the day of Diwali, we wake up early, dress up, and visit family, friends and neighbors to wish them a happy Diwali and new year and to seek blessings. We offer large stainless-steel thali filled with delicious homemade snacks and sweets. Another tradition is to touch the feet of our elders, who then bless us with money as a Diwali gift. We return home with full stomachs and pockets. As children, my siblings and I enjoyed this tradition, which is very similar to trick-or-treating in America.

MAKES 1 GHUGHRA PIE

2 tsp ghee
30g/1oz cashew nuts, chopped
30g/1oz almonds, chopped
30g/1oz pistachios
170g/6oz solid milk (khoya/ mawa), crumbled. (If you don't find khoya/mawa, milk powder can be used as a substitute by mixing 120g/4¼oz/1 cup of milk powder with 4 tbsp of double/heavy cream until it becomes smooth.
60g/2oz icing/confectioners' sugar
½ tsp ground cardamom
8–10 saffron threads, crushed
1½ tsp charoli (optional)
25g/1oz raisins
1 × 23cm/9in pie crust (thawed, if frozen)
1½ tbsp edible rose petals, to garnish
1 tsp poppy seeds, to garnish

Bake the pie crust according to the package instructions – if it requires cooking – then remove it from the oven and let it cool. Turn the oven down to 150°C/300°F/Gas 2.

To prepare the filling, heat the ghee in a non-stick saucepan over a low heat and add all the chopped nuts. Cook for 2–3 minutes, stirring constantly to prevent them from turning too dark. Transfer the nuts to a bowl.

Add the khoya, sugar, cardamom, saffron, charoli, if using, and raisins, and mix together until well combined.

Transfer the prepared filling to the pie crust and gently press it to flatten and smooth the top. Sprinkle rose petals and poppy seeds on top of the pie, then place it on a baking tray. Bake for 8–10 minutes.

Remove the pie from the oven and allow to cool before serving.

Drinks

Rose Lassi

Rose lassi stole my heart when I tried it for the first time in London at my go-to restaurant. Enhanced with rose syrup and adorned with rose petals, this lassi boasts a captivating appearance. It's super addictive. I ordered one glass, and I found myself reaching for two or more!

SERVES 4

730g/1lb 10oz/3 cups full-fat yogurt

6 tbsp rose syrup, readily available in Indian supermarkets

8 tbsp sugar

24 ice cubes

4 tbsp shelled pistachios, slightly crushed, to garnish

4 tbsp cashew nuts, roughly chopped, to garnish

1 tsp dried edible rose petals, to garnish

Combine 480ml/16fl oz/2 cups of water with the yogurt, rose syrup and sugar in a bowl and whisk well until the mixture is fully incorporated.

Add 6 ice cubes to each glass. Divide the mixture between the glasses and garnish with the crushed pistachios, chopped cashew nuts and rose petals. Serve chilled.

Buttermilk with Mint

Fuss-free and refreshing, I first tried this buttermilk drink at a wellness program and was immediately drawn to its unique blend of ginger and mint. However, I appreciate this recipe mainly because it features several ingredients that offer various health benefits – for example, drinking buttermilk (chaas) after or during a meal is known to aid digestion.

SERVES 4

1 litre/32fl oz/4 cups buttermilk

2 tsp cumin seeds, toasted

1cm/½in piece of ginger, peeled

10 mint leaves

1 small green chili (optional)

1 tsp salt or black salt

Handful of coriander/cilantro leaves

Ice cubes, to serve (optional)

Combine all the ingredients in a blender and blitz for a minute. Divide between 4 glasses and serve with ice if you prefer it very cold.

Tip: If you don't have any buttermilk, you can replace it with 375ml/13fl oz/1½ cups of plain yogurt and 750ml/26fl oz/3 cups of water.

Indian Gooseberry Drink

Indian gooseberries (amla) are a powerhouse of nutrients. Vitamin C is a natural antioxidant which protects the body from free radicals – it's essential to the body's overall wellbeing.

In addition, amla is very versatile: it can be eaten raw, added to pickles and jams or juiced, as I have done in this refreshing and tangy drink. Drinking diluted amla juice (particularly on an empty stomach) aids digestion and is the ideal morning juice to start the day.

SERVES 4

8 Indian gooseberries, thawed if using frozen, washed, seeds removed

4cm/1½in piece of fresh root ginger, peeled

1 tbsp fennel seeds

4 tsp lime juice

2½ tbsp honey, plus extra to taste

Ice cubes, to serve

Handful of mint leaves, chopped, to serve

Put the gooseberries in a blender with the ginger, fennel seeds and 1 litre/32fl oz/4 cups of cold water and blitz until smooth. Strain the juice, discarding the pulp, and transfer it to a jug.

Mix in the lime juice and honey, adding a bit more honey if you prefer it sweeter.

Serve immediately over ice with mint leaves.

Note: Frozen gooseberries are readily available at Indian supermarkets.

Green Mango Drink
(Keri No Sarbat)

This tasty and rejuvenating Keri No Sorbet – a green mango drink – is simple to prepare and an excellent way to conquer the summer heat. The drink's cooling properties make it an ideal beverage for summer parties in hot countries worldwide, helping people stay cool and hydrated. You won't fully appreciate how wonderful it is until you try it – take a sip, and you'll be hooked.

SERVES 4

2 tbsp cumin seeds

2 medium unripe mangoes, peeled and finely grated

1 tsp salt

4 tbsp sugar

Ice cubes, to serve

To toast the cumin seeds, heat a small heavy-based pan over a low heat. Add the cumin seeds and dry roast them for 2–3 minutes, stirring continuously, until they start to release their aroma. Remove the pan from the heat and let the seeds cool, then grind them in a mortar and pestle or grinder to make a coarse powder.

Combine all the ingredients in a medium-sized bowl and mix until the sugar dissolves. Let the mixture sit for 5 minutes. Add 1 litre/32fl oz/4 cups of water, and mix well.

Strain into a pitcher and add ice cubes. Serve chilled for a refreshing summer drink.

ABOUT THE AUTHOR

Vina Patel's passion is to bring undiscovered, vibrant, and flavorful recipes from the State of Gujarat to the world's kitchens. Gujarat is a state in western India with a population of 60 million.

She holds a degree in accounting from Gujarat's prestigious university. After graduation, she married and immigrated to the US in 1989. While raising three children and supporting my husband's career, she worked for two Silicon Valley start-ups as head of finance and accounting. Later, she earned a second degree in finance from a Silicon Valley's college.

Although she could have continued to pursue a career in Silicon Valley, her desire and passion to feed and teach home-cooked Gujarati food to her young growing family, friends, and business colleagues led her to experiment with hundreds of recipes over 30 years. Vina's passion for cooking and recreating Gujarati dishes, fondly recalled from my childhood, slowly became an obsession.

Vina is the author of *From Gujarat with Love*, which received coverage in *National Geographic Food & Travel*, *Washington Post*, *CBC Canadian Broadcasting Company*, *Times of India*, and *Gujarat Samachar*. Food critic for the *Daily Mail*, Tom Parker Bowles, selected it as a book that will endure long after the latest fads have fizzled and died. The book was also nominated as a finalist for the Edward Stanford Travel Writing Award.

ACKNOWLEDGMENTS

The Spice Collector's Cookbook is truly a family affair. My family have been my biggest supporters and cheerleaders throughout my culinary journey. Behind every successful man, there is a woman. However, in my case, there is a man – my kind and loving husband – and my children. My family is everything to me. They always stand by me like a rock! I am immensely grateful for their love and encouragement and for bringing lots of love and happiness to me! You are the reason I am standing here and being where I want to be.

The driving force behind my book began with my world's best daughter, Elissa, nicknamed Ella Bella, Elia and Bablu. She was only four years old when a friend asked her what her favorite food was and, without hesitation, she replied, "My mom's food". Her innocent comment warmed my heart; it was one of the best feelings I've ever had. I never would have guessed that her sweet comment would inspire me to write cookbooks one day, both for my family and the world. Her idea to write a cookbook was a game-changer for me, the catalyst in shaping my culinary journey. Elissa, you are a star of the show, and now I've published two cookbooks! I am extremely grateful for your encouragement. You are the most caring and sweetheart daughter with a heart of gold. I don't know what I did to deserve you, but I thank God every

"I must have asked God to give me a family who will always love me, and he gave me Haresh, Elissa, Aamir and Ravina."

day for you. You even helped me design the book cover. Your ability to locate the perfect accessories and props, and your attention to every detail was truly admirable. You did an outstanding job, dear artist daughter. Your attention to detail and artistic talent brought the cover to life and made it a treasured item that will be cherished for generations.

Writing a cookbook has brought me so much happiness, and I owe it all to my sweetheart daughter and designer, Elissa.

My husband is the hero and the pillar of our family, the Patels. He's always there to help, and I don't know where I would be without his support. He never says no to grocery shopping, even during food photoshoots and testing periods. He sympathizes with my extensive grocery list and goes to multiple stores to keep up with it, despite the number of dirty dishes I create for him in the kitchen. He's a true witness to the amount of work I put into perfecting my recipes. I didn't sleep for the entire months of March and April when I was testing and perfecting my recipes. I'm so grateful that he's there to show his support and appreciate my hard work in creating a great cookbook.

During a week-long food photoshoot, I would cook 9 – 10 dishes a day at the speed of light. I would wake up early in the morning to pack fresh groceries, mostly bought by my husband from the local farmer's markets, and would leave at 5 a.m. to beat the traffic and drive fifty-six miles to the prop studio in Berkeley. Haresh would prepare breakfast for me to ensure that I had something to eat before the photoshoot. It was quite a process and a labor of love. I love how he noticed my hard work and always blessed me, saying, "One day, you will be so successful. I and the universe are watching everything you do to create not just a cookbook, but a great cookbook."

My best memories – which I often mention to him – are of how much time he has dedicated to helping me rock the cookbook author panel. I like how he supports everything I do. Besides enjoying my food as a fan, he also takes on the role of a food critic. During food testing, I allow him to criticize my food, and that is the only time I allow him to criticize my food! Thank you so much for always being there for me and believing in me. You are always positive and have taught me how to stay positive at all times. None of this would have been possible without your trust in me. You will be remembered by me and the world, not only as a successful man of Silicon Valley, but also as a supportive husband who played the best supporting role.

Whenever my son Aamir enjoys one of my dishes, he always says "Don't change the recipe!" He insists that I maintain consistency in my recipe whenever he requests his favorite dinner. I am thankful for his strong opinion in preserving my recipes. Whenever he likes something I cook, he calls me to express his appreciation. Aamir and I often have discussions about food ventures and politics. His entrepreneurial spirit adds an exciting twist to my culinary journey, which leads to innovative ideas and exciting food ventures. He is a true entrepreneur and infuses his innovative spirit into everything I cook. I can see clearly that his love for my food shines through in every conversation he has with others. He enjoys showing off my cookbook to his friends and bragging about my cooking skills. I appreciate his non-stop support and valuable advice on not living in fear. Thank you to my one and only Aamir.

The youngest and most adorable member of our family, Ravina, recently discovered her passion for cooking my recipes. She has been showcasing her culinary skills using recipes passed down through generations. I am proud to announce that we have a new master chef in the kitchen. Ravina's texts about how she enjoys my recipes in her off-campus kitchen inspire many of us. I am thankful for her encouragement to prioritize home-cooked meals.

Ravina is simply perfect in every way. Despite her busy schedule with exams and other obligations, she still finds time to cook and often prepares enough food for 2 – 3 days. Her friends are often caught eating her delicious leftovers.

I welcome students from around the world to try my recipes. Ravina often says, "Mom, I love cooking at home, and your recipes make it easy to do so. The satisfaction of a home-cooked meal is unparalleled." It brings me joy to watch her savor the food, especially when it helps her feel less homesick. I am excited to spend more time cooking together in our Bay Area kitchen. Thank you so much for sharing your love and joy for cooking with me, lovingly nicknamed Bubz.

The Spice Collector's Cookbook is truly a family cookbook, and I owe my success to my loved ones. I am grateful to God for creating such wonderful things in this world, but most importantly, for blessing me with a caring and loving family. Thank you for being my guiding light, my source of inspiration, and the reason behind my smile. I love you more!

I am forever grateful to Monica Meehan. I am so lucky to have her as part of the wonderful team and as my culinary agent. Her invaluable assistance in bringing my recipes to life, her kind support, and her extensive knowledge of the industry have been instrumental in my success. I vividly remember being in New Delhi when she informed me that she had found the perfect home for my manuscript.

Jonathan Lovekin is a renowned photographer with whom I had the pleasure of working on both of my cookbooks. Jonathan's photography skills are truly god-given. He often compliments my food, which is a big deal coming from one of the world's best photographers. Jonathan, I am incredibly grateful for everything you have done. It's heartwarming to see that there is still so much goodness in the world, and every time I think of you, I feel that way. I feel honored and blessed to collaborate with such a renowned photographer in the industry.

To Ella Chappell, I would like to express my gratitude for all the happy moments you have created for me and my family. Your flexibility, respect, and inclusivity in every decision we made in creating this cookbook mean so much to us. I particularly appreciate the time you took to talk over the phone when needed and your patience with the book cover. Working with you has been an absolute pleasure. I'm very grateful that you have shown kindness and professionalism throughout our collaboration. You handled everything with ease and your kind nature put me at ease. Thank you once again for everything. You are a true team player.

Thank you to Mummy and Pappa for being such big fans of my food. Your presence is always felt, every time I cook your favorite dish. I feel very special, as you created such a nurturing and carefree environment for me, allowing me to be *me*, letting me thrive independently, and instilling in me a sense of confidence and trust in everything. You have been a constant source of strength to this date.

I know you would be immensely proud of me, and I wish you were here to witness my achievements. Nevertheless, I find great peace in knowing that you watch over me from above, blessing me with your love.

To my beloved two elder brothers, whose untimely departure still leaves a void in our family. The last time I saw my eldest brother was in 2019 when I went to India for a photoshoot for my first cookbook *From Gujarat With Love*. We celebrated Rakshabandhan together over my favorite sweets and dinner. I gave him a big hug just before my departure. It was a fun time, and I left with great memories. However, I did not know it would be our last hug, and these precious moments would become scars, as it was the most unexpected loss. Bhai, since this marked our last observance of this sacred brother-sister bonding tradition, I cherish this festival and celebrate the beautiful memories with you by keeping you in my thoughts. His last text to me was "Babul Ki Duayen Leti Ja," which means, "Take your father's blessings." Thank you for leaving true blessings behind for me.

I cherish the memories of your warm hospitality whenever we gathered and all the meals and parties on the open terrace of our house we shared.

I'm proud to share my passion for cooking and family recipes with the world. And this is the power of food that always brings us together.

My first cookbook, *From Gujarat With Love*, has brought lots of smiles to my fans and created memorable stories. I can't wait for *The Spice Collector's Cookbook* to bring joy to the world.

Index